THE COMPOSER'S TOOLKIT

Classical techniques for modern musicians

Christopher Tarrant and Natalie Wild

© 2026 by Faber Music Ltd
This edition first published in 2026
Brownlow Yard, 12 Roger Street, London WC1N 2JU
Cover & layout design by Liz Ogden
Music setting by John Rogers
Printed in England by Caligraving Ltd
All rights reserved

ISBN10: 0-571-54351-0
EAN13: 978-0-571-54351-9

To buy Faber Music publications or to find out about the full range of titles available
please contact your local music retailer or Faber Music sales enquiries:

Faber Music Ltd, Burnt Mill, Elizabeth Way, Harlow CM20 2HX
Tel: +44 (0) 1279 82 89 82
fabermusic.com

For Jasper

PREFACE

Creating music has always been a craft. It is a skill that involves hard work, technique, and crucially, the use of materials *that already exist.* This book challenges the idea that composition relies on unpredictable bursts of inspiration. Instead, it shows how you can create your own music through careful and methodical stages. The techniques covered in this book will help you to unlock your creativity, guiding you from simple sketches to fully formed, polished compositions.

Composers in the eighteenth century rarely sat down and wrote music from start to finish. Instead, they often improvised at their instrument and then wrote down their improvisations. In order to do this effectively, young musicians were taught **schemata** – basic musical shapes that were widely used and recognised. These schemata can be arranged, rearranged, decorated, and put together to create unique pieces of music.

Schemata are like building blocks that can help you shape and organise your ideas. This book will begin by introducing some of these basic musical shapes and show you how to use them to build short pieces of music. This isn't about following a rigid formula – it's about giving you the tools to be creative with pre-existing musical materials. You'll have the freedom to combine and develop these ideas in your own way, just like a chef or a builder might use their ingredients or materials to create something new and original. As you explore these patterns yourself, you'll learn how to turn your initial musical improvisations and sketches into full musical scores with depth and direction – something structured, interesting, expressive, and unique.

How to use this book

This book is arranged into three parts, each focusing on a key aspect of the compositional process. While it can be worked through methodically from start to finish, it can also be used for more casual reference depending on prior experience of composing, or even used as a guide for refining existing compositions.

PART I: introduces some of the most common **schemata** – the musical shapes that form the starting point for improvisation and composition.

It is useful to become fully acquainted with these in isolation so the shapes are familiar enough to improvise around. The idea of composition taking place in front of a computer or piece of manuscript paper should be rejected to begin with. Instead it is good practice simply to play the different schema patterns in a key that works best for your instrument (e.g. a violinist might use an open-string key such as D major) in their most basic outline, getting used to physical and aural engagement with them. Very soon, this will organically lead to improvisation around the shapes.

By the end of **Part I**, you will have composed a simple rounded binary form piece – a two-section composition that lays the foundation for further development.

PART II: explores how to take the rounded binary form piece from **Part I** and transform it into a variety of larger musical forms.

You can approach **Part II** by using your piece as a section in a larger form (theme and variations, minuet and trio, or rondo). Each of these has different challenges, so think about which feels most comfortable to you. **Part II** also introduces schemata that have not yet been covered as a means of expanding the form you have settled on, combining these with other compositional techniques to add character and individuality to your music.

By the end of **Part II**, you will have a complete score of a full piece of music, following one of the musical forms covered in this section and closing the music appropriately using cadences.

PART III: introduces ways to enrich your composition at a much more detailed level. These developments form the bridge between short, functional patterns and more expansive musical forms. While the basic versions of each schema are perfectly usable as they are, elaboration allows you to bring variety, personality, and style to your music.

Responding to a composition brief sets out a methodical approach to writing to brief, taking into account all of the tools that are covered in **Parts I–III**.

Appendix 3 sets out some schematic pathways that offer some alternative starting points for your composition. You may start improvising on some schemata and find that your own imagination takes you somewhere completely different!

Guidance for teachers

The aim of this book is to dismantle the barriers that are encountered when teaching composition in schools.

The approach outlined in this book is designed to be both accessible and aspirational, enabling teachers to integrate composition into a comprehensive and well-rounded music curriculum rooted in a solid understanding of musical fundamentals. While a grasp of music notation is preferable, it is by no means essential – these techniques can be taught aurally.

Drawing on Robert O. Gjerdingen's landmark publication *Music in the Galant Style*[1] as well as the authors' extensive experience in secondary schools across the UK, the techniques outlined in this book mitigate against common pitfalls in student compositions, such as:

- Low-register triads
- Over-reliance on four-chord loops
- Chord progressions with limited scope for development
- Disjunct melodies derived from chords
- A lack of melodic direction
- Overly complex textures with excessive layering

---

[1] (Oxford University Press, 2007)

In order to be able to compose successfully, students need to be able to improvise. It is common to experience improvisation by starting with creating some sounds on the spot, before moving on to ordering those sounds using a predetermined framework (such as a pentatonic scale in blues improvisation). However, it is difficult to know how to progress to feeling confident in creating a fully formed, well-structured, and effective composition from those basic starting points. This book provides a framework in the form of schemata, the same teaching that allowed orphans in seventeenth-century Naples to learn a trade at the first conservatories and become elite composers. The method we explore suggests ways in which students can expand, order, and embellish their ideas. It therefore equips them with the tools needed to confidently and stylishly create a full score from those early sketches, resulting in a skill set that is far greater than the sum of its parts.

Christopher Tarrant and Natalie Wild

A Spotify playlist containing the musical
examples referenced throughout the book
is available via the QR code and link below:
https://bit.ly/ComposersToolkit

CONTENTS

INTRODUCTION

Where does music come from and how is it created?

Discussion about composition nowadays often relies on some quite old-fashioned ideas. We only have to switch on the radio to hear talk of a composer's 'timeless genius', with presenters and pundits referring to individual pieces as though they were the result of a burst of divine inspiration that could only have been harnessed by a uniquely gifted person. Music is regularly discussed in terms of 'inspiration', 'expression', 'emotion', and 'genius'. Artistic depictions reinforce these ideas, showing the composer in a dream world, or in nature, or relying on divine intervention.

These terms don't come from music or musicians themselves, but from a nineteenth-century myth about how music is made. This book sets out to show that creativity isn't just about mysterious flashes of inspiration or genius (if that were the case, most of us would be ruled out before we even started). It also challenges the idea that expression and emotion are critically important to music, but that they are not always the goal or the starting point of the compositional process, nor do they have to arrive in a sudden burst of inspiration.

Let's consider carefully the role of emotion in the act of composition. It is unlikely that composers such as J.S. Bach (1685–1750) or Miles Davis (1926–1991) created music that directly mirrored their transient moods. Either side of the Romantic era (which we define very loosely – let's say the 'long' nineteenth century, roughly 1789–1914) there were many composers who approached music as a job to be done, in a similar way to any other trained craftsman. Even Romantic composers did not think of their own creative work as being solely reliant on unpredictable bursts of emotion or inspiration. Brahms wrote in 1876 (the year of the first performance of his first symphony, now a central work of the Romantic repertoire):

There is no such thing as *creating*, without hard work. That which you would call invention, that is to say, a thought, an idea, is simply an inspiration from above, for which I am not responsible, which is no merit of mine. Yea, it is a present, a gift, which I ought even to despise until I have made it my own by right of hard work.[2]

Top right: *Beethoven Composing the Pastoral Symphony* by Franz Hegi
Bottom left: *Allegory of Beethoven as a Musical Genius* by Sigmund Walter *Hampel*
[2] *Recollections of Brahms*, Albert Dietrich and J.V. Widmann (Palala Press, 2015).

Although this comment might appear stereotypically Romantic at first, the sensibility comes from an earlier age when composers drew on a common stock of musical ideas. The word 'compose' literally means to 'put together' (*com* + *posare*), and eighteenth-century composers had access to stock musical phrases. It was their job not so much to invent new ideas as to assemble, arrange, combine and embellish these materials, much like a carpenter crafting furniture from pre-cut wood. Stock musical phrases were commonly owned by the composers, performers, and listeners who engaged what we now call the **galant style**. This style straddles the late Baroque (represented in the music of J.S. Bach and Handel) and the Classical period (represented in Vienna by Haydn, Mozart, and Beethoven).

The importance of improvisation

The galant style relies above all on the practice of **improvisation**. Today when we play a piece by an eighteenth-century composer, let's say a sonata by Haydn, we think of it as a finished work. In reality, the written score is often merely a snapshot of an improvisation that the composer has captured through notation at a certain point in the creative process. It would have been normal for composers during this time to work at the keyboard, improvising ideas and notating them.

Improvisation can cause anxiety among musicians who are used to performing from a notated score. How is it possible to compose music in real time as you are playing it? There are some styles of music which much more obviously lend themselves to improvisation. Some types of jazz, for example, rely heavily on improvised solos. Improvisation also plays an important part in much folk music and non-Western musical traditions, for example the Eastern European folk, Indian classical, and Middle Eastern traditions. Though less obvious because of its more prescriptive

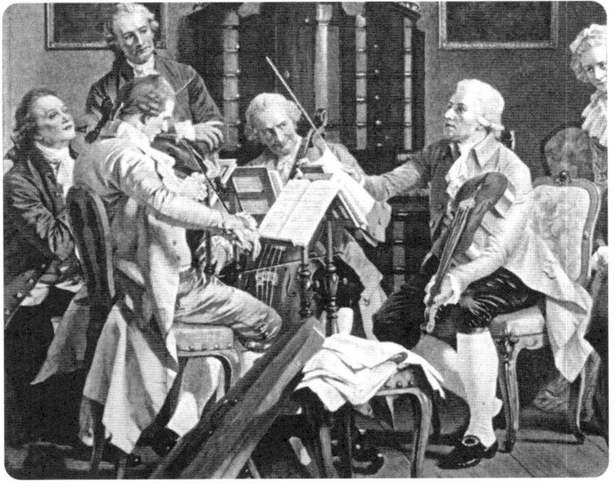

practice of notation, European classical music is built on a process comparable with these genres – a process of improvising on basic musical shapes. So, for European composers of the eighteenth century such as Handel, Vivaldi, J.S. Bach, Haydn, and Mozart, creating new pieces of music was about writing down improvisations.

But if improvising is about turning a basic idea into a more complex one, where do these basic shapes come from? The answer is not that they fall from the sky, as Brahms might imply. These basic shapes were all around and were regularly taught in music schools – conservatories. Musical invention often began with adapting shared, well-known patterns rather than starting from nothing. The same principle applies to composers today, whatever their style. Whether writing a song,

Top left: *Ludwig van Beethoven Dreaming at the Keyboard* by Aimé de Lemud
Bottom right: *Haydn Playing Quartets* by Julius Schmid

film cue, jazz chart, or symphonic piece, creativity often begins with recognising and reshaping familiar patterns into something personal and new. It is this method that we will explore throughout this book, finding ways to embed and manipulate these shapes into our own compositions.

TERMS OF REFERENCE

In this book we will be using a very simple system of notation to describe each schema, as detailed by Gjerdingen.[3] While we will frequently demonstrate ideas using conventional staff notation, each schema can be expressed in different tempi, metres, keys, registers, and timbres. So, when speaking in general terms we use the following system of numbers which relate to degrees of the scale:

- Melody notes are represented by numbers in black circles. So, the tonic is represented using the number ❶, for example. The 'Do-Re-Mi' schema (which we will come to later), is expressed like this: ❶-❷-❸.

- Bass notes are represented using numbers in white circles. The bass line of a perfect cadence is represented like this: ⑤-①.

- A musical shape that is represented only by using scale degrees is called a **schema** (the plural is **schemata**).

- All of the schemata we will look at consist of two parts: bass line and a melody line. At this stage, we are not focusing on chords or harmony; these ideas can be developed later. Instead, we are learning to write simple two-part counterpoint with the melody and bass working together.

[3] Robert O. Gjerdingen, *Music in the Galant Style* (New York: Oxford University Press, 2007).

[T]he great doesn't happen through impulse alone …
[it] is a succession of little things that are brought together.

–Vincent van Gogh

PART I: MUSICAL MATERIALS

Most pieces of music are made up of a melody, a bass line, and some harmony filling out the texture. This is true of most kinds of tonal music. As we start composing, it is important that we have a checklist to refer back to:

What makes a good melody?

At its heart, a good composition needs a good melody – that is, one that moves with clarity and direction, holding the interest of the listener without too many surprises.

- Does the melody have a clear, recognisable line?
- Does the melody move in steps with occasional leaps?
- Does the melody have some rhythmic variety to keep it interesting?

What goes with a good melody?

Along with your melody, you need a bass line to support it. We need to keep the following in mind:

- Is there a clear bass line that underpins the melody?
- Is there a combination of similar and contrary motion between the melody and bass line?
- Is there a clear sense of implied harmony, where the combination of the melody and bass suggests a harmony, even if the chords haven't been written out?

How were famous composers taught to compose?

But where do these good melodies come from? For many eighteenth-century musicians, the answer was in a common stock of patterns passed down through teaching traditions. The earliest *conservatories* were set up in the port city of Naples, where the large number of abandoned children meant that a lot of orphanages were established there. Orphans were usually taught a trade in these institutions so that they wouldn't be destitute as adults. They were looked after, given food and shelter – they were 'conserved' here (which is where the Italian term *conservatorio* and the French *conservatoire* derive from). During the nineteenth century conservatories began to appear in northern Europe, famously in Paris and Leipzig, where many of the most successful musicians of the nineteenth and twentieth centuries were trained.

The orphans at these institutions were taught, first and foremost, to improvise. Improvisation in this tradition did not begin with silence, or a blank sheet of paper. Instead, children were taught some of the most commonly used basic ideas in the European tradition until they were familiar enough to refer to, play, and improvise around. We refer to each of these basic ideas as a **schema**.

These shapes, or **schemata**, can be used flexibly, combined, rearranged, decorated, and developed, in order to construct the framework of a piece of music. Of course, sometimes a composer will have to come up with something new, but much of this repertoire is built like a patchwork quilt of schemata that were ready to hand. Some of the schemata might be new to you, but it's likely that you'll recognise many of them, perhaps never having realised that they had a name!

Once we have introduced some of these basic shapes, we'll show you how to order and combine them into short pieces of music – a framework that you can then embellish, decorate, and *improvise* on. The process is not meant to be a rigid 'paint by numbers' approach, but an invitation for you to come up with something creative from some pre-existing materials. In fact, in each task you are encouraged to try something different if the process of improvising around the materials takes you there! Imagine the way a chef cooks a meal. The chef doesn't have to grow each individual ingredient – they are ready for him in the kitchen. Although these schemata were used in the eighteenth century, they describe patterns of motion and expectation that underpin much tonal and modal music today. Film scores, musicals, jazz standards, and pop music all use these shapes, consciously or not.

This section will begin by introducing three of the most versatile schemata in the style, along with a strategy for arranging these ideas into a form. By the end of **Part I** you should be able to construct a simple piece of music. We will start with one of the most instantly recognisable shapes in the repertoire.

OPENING SCHEMA: THE ROMANESCA

There are several different types of musical patterns that could be used to begin a composition. They vary in length but are usually a bar or two long, and they establish the key and provide a main idea for the piece of music.

Of all the musical ideas that circulated in the eighteenth century, the **Romanesca** was one of the most versatile. It was most frequently used as an opening idea which could be varied and developed in several different ways.

The 'leaping-bass' Romanesca

The most basic form, the 'leaping-bass' Romanesca, is built on a simple pattern in the bass voice. Let's look at it in C major: It starts on the tonic, C, then leaps down a fourth to G (the fifth degree), steps up a second to A (the sixth degree), leaps down a fourth to E (the third degree), steps up a second to F (the fourth degree), and so on.

This motion in the bass line – ①-⑤-⑥-③ – is a progression of tension and release that is found in lots of different kinds of music, from classical pieces to pop ballads to jazz standards. To accompany this bass line, composers often wrote a melody beginning on ❸ and then descending by step, with one melody note to go with each note in the bass. This results in a series of root-position chords which eventually arrive back at the tonic.

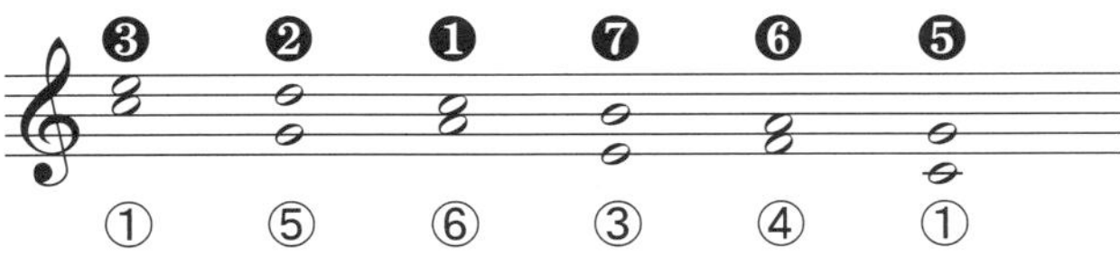

This pattern might be recognisable to you if you have heard Pachelbel's *Canon in D*, in which he modifies the melody at the end of the phrase in order to maintain the continuity of the music.

Pachelbel: *Canon in D*

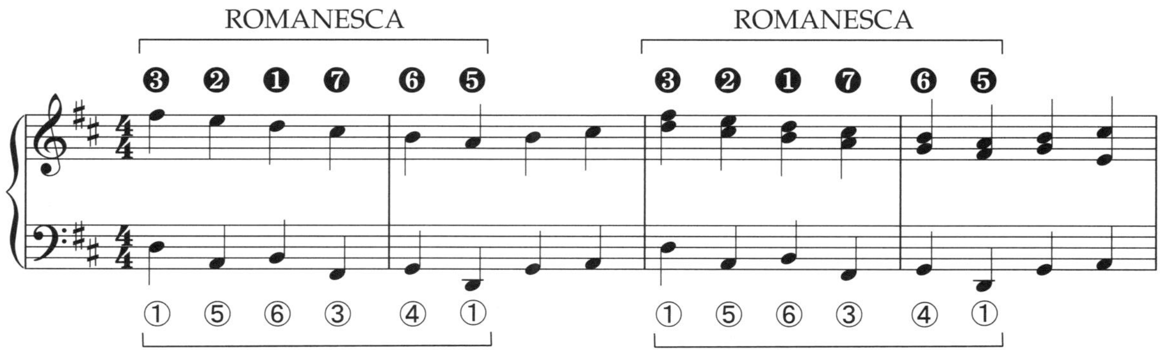

The 'stepwise-bass' Romanesca

The 'leaping-bass' Romanesca was the most basic option but there is also a 'stepwise-bass' version in which the bass simply moves down by a step. This produces a pattern of alternating root-position and first inversion chords, which are indicated by figured bass:

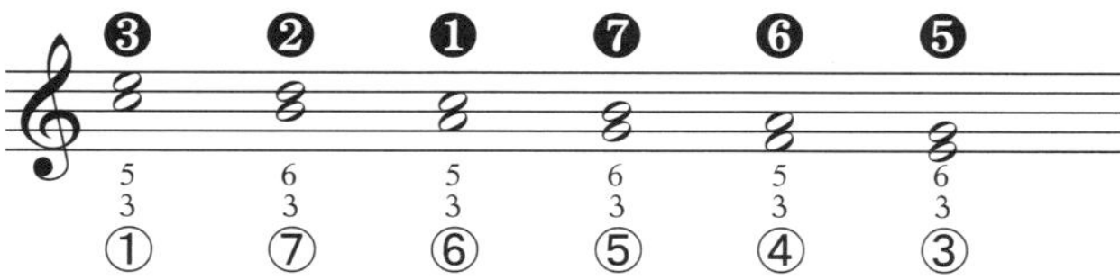

> ## Figured bass recap
>
> The numbers describe the intervals above the bass note which tell you the chord's inversion:
> Let's take C major as an example:
>
> - 5/3 – **Root position:** the bass is the root (C). Above it you hear a 3rd and a 5th (e.g. C–E–G).
>
> - 6/3 – **1st inversion:** the bass is the 3rd of the chord (E). Above it you hear a 3rd and a 6th (e.g. E–G–C).
>
> - 6/4 – **2nd inversion:** the bass is the 5th (G). Above it you hear a 4th and a 6th (e.g. G–C–E).

Musical references:
Pachelbel, Johann: *Canon in D,* bars 3–6

The Galant Romanesca

The most common version of the Romanesca in the eighteenth century, though, combines the two strategies, with the bass moving in step to begin with, before leaping down at the end producing the bass line ①–⑦–⑥–③. Let's call this the **galant Romanesca**.

The melody in the galant Romanesca usually focuses on a mixture of combinations of ❶ and ❺. Some of the main variants are shown below in the key of C major:

Variants of the galant Romanesca

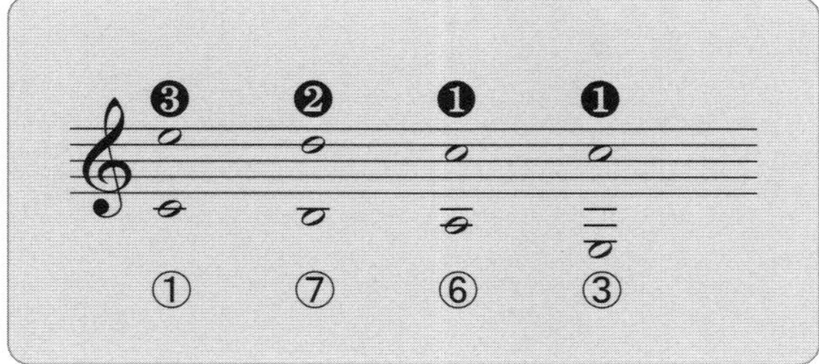

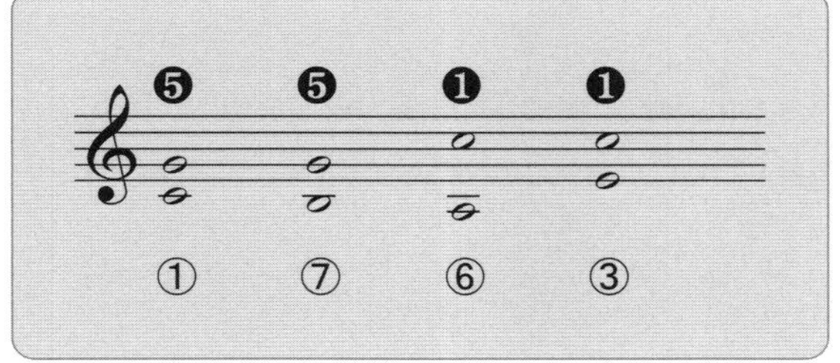

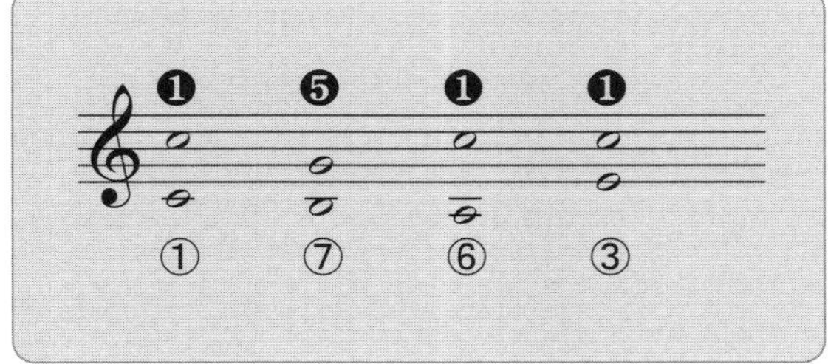

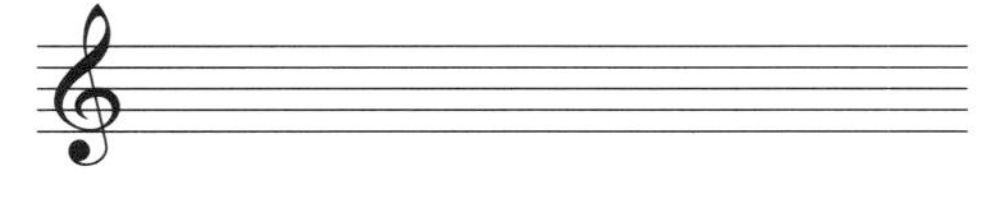

The Romanesca in action

We have seen how to start a piece using the Romanesca as an opening schema. Although this method of composing originated as a way of creating Western classical music, it is certainly not restricted to this. The Romanesca's descending shape clearly outlines the key while providing a sense of nostalgia. Let's look at some examples from the Western classical, pop, and jazz traditions.

It is worth noting that Mozart was no more than 8 years old when he wrote this and had clearly been taught the basic shapes of the galant style!

The Romanesca in popular music

There are countless examples of the Romanesca as an opening idea in popular music. Here are just four from the jazz, pop, rock, and folk traditions:

Billy Taylor, *I Wish I Knew How It Would Feel to Be Free*: first four bars [0:00–0:09]

In this jazz standard written by Billy Taylor, the Romanesca pattern opens the song but with a sharpened ⑤ to give a more jazzy feel.

Oasis, *Don't Look Back in Anger*: chorus [1:10–1:32]

As with most of these examples, the Romanesca pattern (which can be heard in both the verse and chorus) follows the leaping bass path of ①-⑤-⑥-③ before moving to a cadence. We will explore how to do this later in the chapter.

Green Day, *Basket Case*: verse [0:00–0:22]

In this American rock classic, the Romanesca is heard more fully, with the ①-⑤-⑥-③ pattern being followed by ④-①-⑤.

Ralph McTell, *Streets of London*: intro [0:00–0:11]

In this example the ①-⑤-⑥-③ Romanesca can be heard clearly in the intro, as well as in the verses.

As you can hear in these examples, the Romanesca can fit many styles once you start to play around with it. We will explore ways to adapt this schema for your own composition in **Part III**.

Musical references:
Mozart, W. A.: *Sonata for Keyboard and Violin*, K.7, Adagio, bars 1–2

A piece in progress

Throughout this book we will develop a model composition based on the ideas and patterns we explore. Use this working example as a guide to see how the techniques can work in practice. As you study the model and begin your own sketches, keep the following in mind:

- Play the examples on your own instrument so you can hear them, as well as see the patterns on paper.

- Use the working example as guidance, but make your own creative decisions.

- Less is more – don't rush to complicate the patterns.

- Don't be afraid to change your mind. If you don't like what you hear, change it!

- Always refer back to the checklist of criteria for what makes a good composition on page 12.

TOOLKIT: A WORKING EXAMPLE 

Step 1

We decided to compose in $\frac{2}{4}$ and in the key of **C major**, and we opted for a **galant Romanesca** for our opening schema.

Our outline looks like this:

Step 2

After improvising further, we added some extra notes to fill out the harmony in the middle.

- The first note of the Romanesca is a G, supported by C in the bass. This is a root-position C major chord, so we added the missing E into the inner voice.

- The second note is still a G, but with a B in the bass. This makes a G major chord in first inversion, so we added the missing note from the G major triad, D, into the inner voice, keeping the motion from one note to the next as smooth as possible.

- The third melody note is a C, supported by an A in the bass. This makes an A minor triad, so we added the missing note to complete the harmony: E.

- The final melody note of the Romanesca is also a C, this time supported by an E in the bass. This makes a first inversion C major chord. We added a C to the inner voice here to keep the part writing smooth.

Step 3

Following the previous steps meant that we had already fulfilled some of the criteria outlined at the start of **Part I**:

- Is there a combination of similar and contrary motion between the melody and bass lines? ✓
- Is there a clear sense of implied harmony? ✓

We then decided to improvise some more around this to get something a bit more interesting. We referred back to our checklist, made sure that the original notes stayed in place and avoided moving too far away from them to keep the melody mainly conjunct with occasional leaps.

- Does the melody have a clear, recognisable line? ✓
- Does the melody move in steps with occasional leaps? ✓

We opted to add dotted rhythms for variety, and decided to keep our bass line the same to avoid overcomplicating it.

- Does the melody have some rhythmic variety to keep it interesting? ✓
- Is there a clear bass line that underpins the melody? ✓

TASK

1. Decide on a time signature

$\frac{2}{4}$ and $\frac{3}{4}$ are particularly Classical, and $\frac{2}{4}$ is probably the most straightforward one to begin with as it avoids having to stretch different events of the pattern out for too long.

$\frac{4}{4}$ is good for many styles of music, especially pop and rock.

2. Decide on a key

Pick a key that you can improvise in comfortably on your main instrument. Remember, you can always transpose your material into a different key later if you want.

3. Start to play around with the Romanesca to develop it:

- Keep the notes the same, but change the rhythm.
- Introduce other notes from the triad to add interest.

TOP TIP

Take your time with the improvisation. Focus on becoming familiar with the schema outline first, then add or change notes in time.

Alternative openings to try

The Romanesca is not the only schema you can use to open a piece of music. See below for details of other schemata you can use and where to find them in the book.

Schema	Outline	Usage
Do-Re-Mi See **Part II** – Rondo form	A smooth, step-by-step rise in the melody (**❶**-**❷**-**❸**) supported by simple I and V harmonies.	The ascending melody gives the opening an aspirational, heroic feel
Sol-Fa-Mi See **Appendix 2**	Stepwise descent (**❺**-**❹**-**❸**) in the melody supported by simple tonic and dominant harmonies.	This downward motion would suit a calm or reflective opening.
Meyer See **Part II** – Ternary form	**❶**-**❼** | **❹**-**❸** in the melody supported by ①-② | ⑦-① in the bass.	This creates a sense of tension followed by release, giving the passage forward momentum and expressive shape.
Quiescenza See **Part II** – Expanding your musical form	Stepwise motion in the melody ♭**❼**-**❻**-♮**❼**-**❶** over a tonic pedal	The sustained tonic pedal gives a strong sense of grounding in the key, while the melodic movement creates gentle tension, making this passage ideal for building anticipation.

RESPONDING SCHEMA: THE PRINNER

Now that you know how to open a piece of music, we need something to follow it. As with a conversation, a statement requires a response, and the Prinner was the most common type of musical response in the galant style.

The basic Prinner

The basic version of the Prinner combines two stepwise descending lines, a melody which descends stepwise from ❻ to ❸ and a bass which descends in parallel motion from ④ to ①.

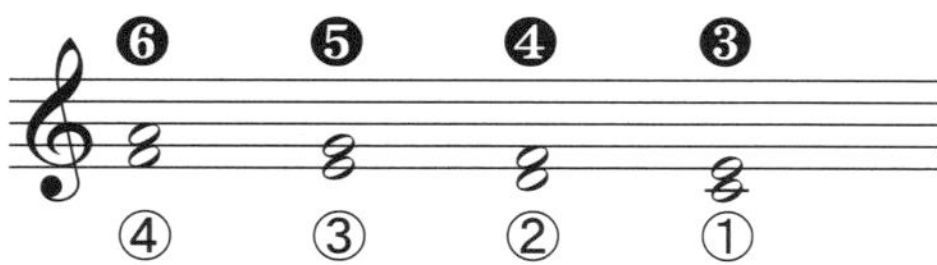

While this basic shape was used thousands of times, composers often added an extra note just before the end, creating a temporary dissonance between bass and melody (an interval of a 7th) and giving the phrase a stronger sense of finality. We will return to this technique when we are ready to use it.

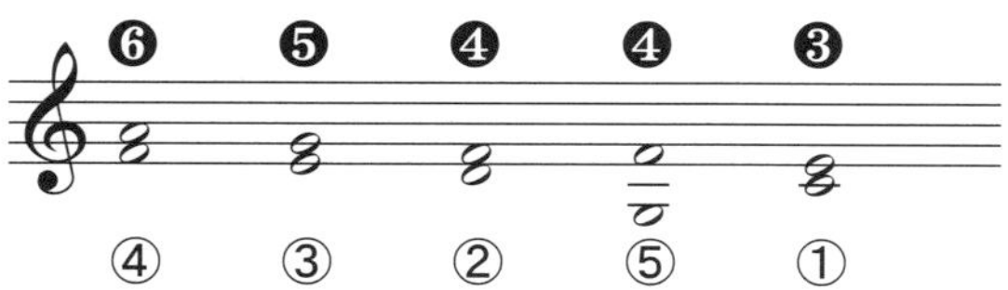

TASK

Try playing both of the Prinner schemata, with and without ⑤ inserted.

The Prinner in video game music

A Prinner can often be found as a responding idea in video game music. It is specifically used in platform games for early game, above-ground, sunny levels, helping to achieve an easy-going, nostalgic mood. In Masato Nakamura's music for *Sonic the Hedgehog* 'Green Hill Zone', the Prinner is used as a response to the opening idea which sits over a tonic pedal.

The Prinner in action

As we shall see later, the Prinner was not only a versatile schema that could appear at various points in a composition, it could also expand and contract to suit different purposes. The next example below is taken from the opening of a piano sonata by Mozart. After the initial idea presented in bars 1–2, Mozart follows with a Prinner in bars 3–4. Here, he adds a high C at the end of bar 3. This note is not part of the schema, but it is consonant with the other notes in the harmony and we therefore understand it as an embellishment of the Prinner.

The next thing Mozart does is to use another Prinner. However, this second Prinner is stretched over the space of four bars, rather than the two-bar Prinner we heard first. The second Prinner also uses a lot of notes to embellish it. Although hardly any of these notes belong to the Prinner schema, we still recognise the shape because the top and bottom notes of each of the scales belong to the schema, and they are connected by stepwise motion.

Musical references:
Nakamura, Masato: *Sonic the Hedgehog (Green Hill Zone Theme)* [0:20–0:26]
Alan Elkins, PhD thesis, *The Development of Musical Style and Ludic Function in Early Video Game Music* (Florida State University, 2023).

Mozart: *Piano Sonata in C Major*

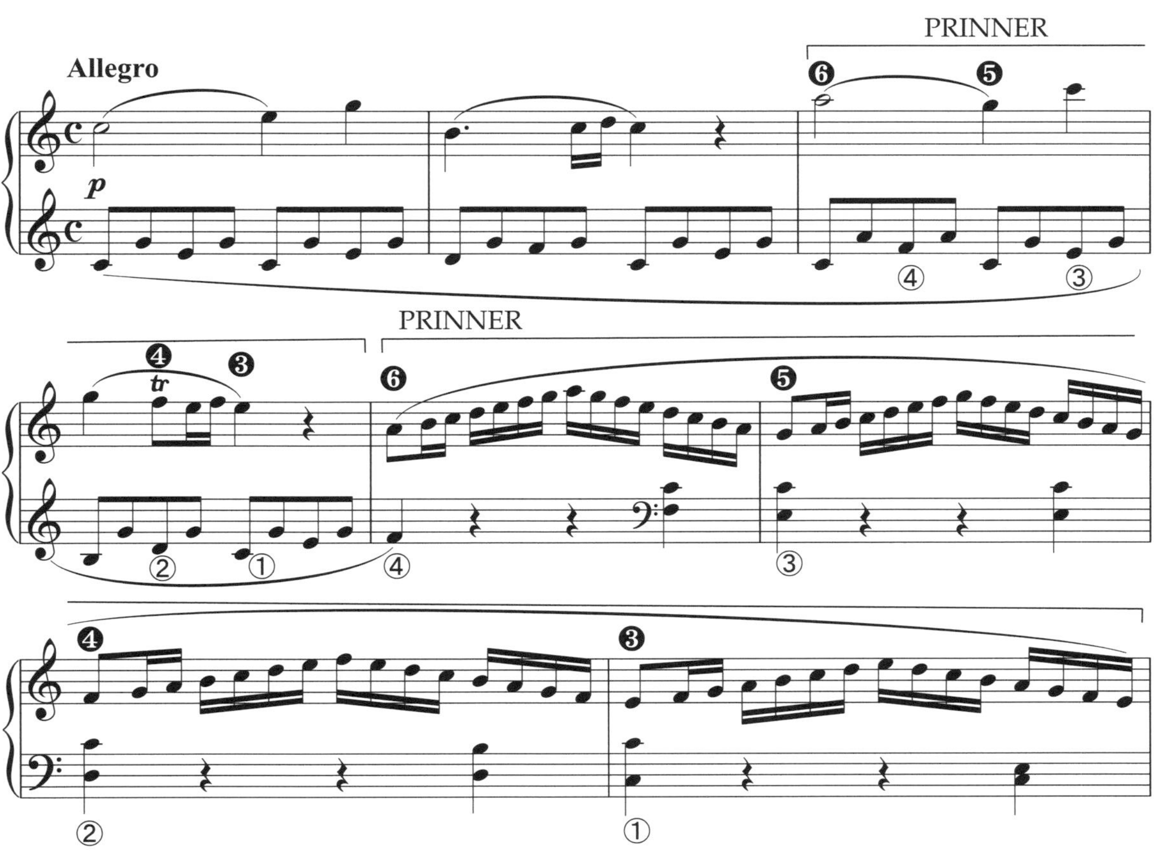

Prinner as contrasting material

While we are primarily exploring the use of the Prinner as a response to an opening idea, there are countless examples of it being used to start a contrasting B section of short pieces of music. This is not limited to Western classical music.

A well-known example can be found in *Rudolph the Red-Nosed Reindeer*, in the contrasting B section: "Then one foggy Christmas Eve, Santa came to say". You can hear the characteristic descending melody and bass lines which outline the Prinner shape.

It is also readily found in music for TV, as heard in the B section to the theme tune for children's TV show *Thomas the Tank Engine*. After the initial material of the A section, contrast is achieved through the use of a Prinner following a descending pattern.

The Prinner is nearly always a *response* to something else. While it is rarely used as an opening gesture (unless used to open a B section), it is common to find it in second place.

Musical references:
Mozart, W. A: *Piano Sonata in C Major, K.545, bars 1–8*
Marks, Johnny: *Rudolph the Red-Nosed Reindeer* [0:34–0:40]
O'Donnell/Campbell: *Thomas Theme* (1984 version) [0:19–0:29]

When you are familiar with the fundamental outline of the Prinner, you can follow your earlier opening Romanesca with this new schema. Here is our working example – as with the Romanesca, use this as guidance for your own creativity. We'll refer back to our composition checklist at each stage.

Step 1 Prinner outline

Our **Prinner outline** is below. You can see we opted to include the ⑤ before the last gesture:

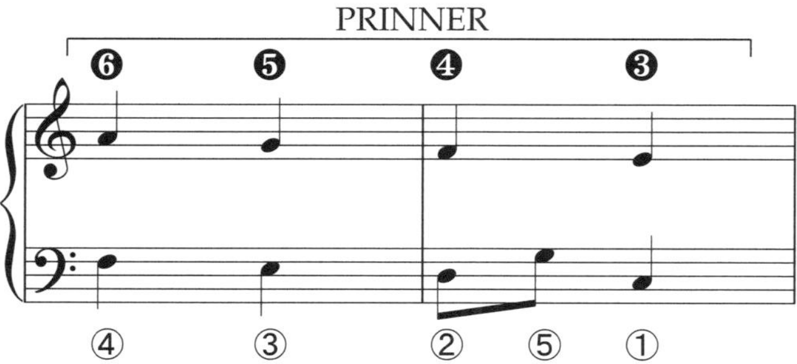

- Is there a clear bass line that underpins the melody? ✓

- Is there a clear sense of implied harmony? ✓

- Is there a combination of similar and contrary motion between the melody and bass lines? ✓

Step 2 Prinner with embellished melody

In order to continue the momentum from our initial schema, we switched to using quavers in the melody:

- Does the melody have a clear, recognisable line? ✓

- Does the melody move in steps with occasional leaps? ✓

Step 3

As with our Romanesca, we then decided to add some notes to flesh out the harmony.

- The first chord is F major in root position. It's missing the fifth of the triad, C, so we added it into the inner voice.

- The second half of the bar, supported by the E in the bass, is a first inversion C major triad, but it is missing the root of the chord, C, so we added this into the inner voice. The inner voice stays on the same note, making the part-writing as smooth as possible.

- The second bar contains a chord with D in the bass, making a dissonance with the G in the melody. The inner voice can play an A – part of the D minor implied harmony.

- The chord with the G in the bass is a dominant seventh. We added a B, which is the third of the chord. D would also have been possible here, but the voices move more smoothly with the B moving by stepwise motion with the notes either side.

- The final chord in this example is a root-position C major triad. G or C are possible here, but G involves jumping, so we chose C for the inner voice so it can continue its stepwise motion to the end of the phrase.

We developed the melody line further, adding a dotted rhythm as well as some harmony notes:

- Does the melody have some rhythmic variety to keep it interesting? ✓

What is a modulation?

In tonal music, modulation is the process of moving from one key to another. Composers of all styles from Baroque to rock use modulation as a structural tool to shift the tonal centre of the music. Traditionally, this can be taught by using chords and exploring how they relate to one another. By using galant schemata, it is very easy to achieve a modulation without worrying about harmonies – the patterns do it for you!

The modulating Prinner

One of the most useful characteristics of the Prinner is its ability to smoothly move from one key to another. In most cases this means a motion from the tonic key (where the music started) to the key of the dominant. This is straightforward to achieve:

- Start your modulating Prinner with ④ in the bass and ❻ in the melody, but notating *in the key that you want to go to*.
    - If you are moving from C major to its dominant G major, your modulating Prinner will start with C in the bass (④) and E (❻) in the melody

- Continue the Prinner steps from this point, descending in both voices until you reach the new key.
    - If you are moving from C major to its dominant G major, your bass line will move in steps from C down to G, with the option of adding a D (⑤) before the G

    - The melody will move in steps from E down to B

You will find that ❸ in the old key is the same note as ❻ in the new key. Likewise, ① in the old key is the same as ④ in the new key. By the time your Prinner has completed its downward journey you will find that the music has automatically arrived in the dominant key, and you can confirm this by adding the leading note (❼) of the new key in an inner voice above ⑤ in the bass. If you have moved from C major to G major, this means adding an F♯!

TOOLKIT: A WORKING EXAMPLE

Let's see what adding a modulating Prinner looks like in our working example.

Step 1 Modulating Prinner outline

We mapped out a modulating Prinner arriving in the 'new' dominant key, G major:

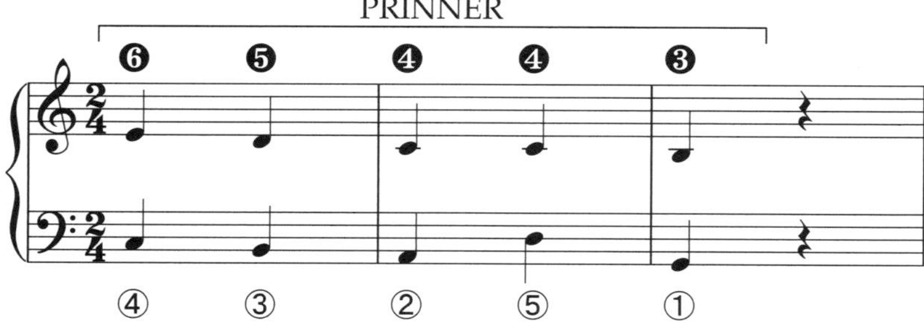

- Is there a clear bass line that underpins the melody? ✓
- Is there a clear sense of implied harmony? ✓

Step 2 Modulating Prinner + decorated melody and harmony

We wanted to keep the energy up so added quavers to the melody line. We also added some harmony notes to reinforce the modulation:

- The first chord is a C major root-position triad, so we added the missing G. The second is a G major first-inversion triad, so we added the missing G. This makes good, smooth part writing.

- In the second bar, the inner voice adds another note that fits the A minor harmony, then moves step by step through a brief clash (G) before resolving to F♯. This is called a *passing note* (or *passing dissonance*). Passing notes move by step and the dissonance should be on a weak beat.

- The F♯ is the leading note of G major. Together with the D in the bass, it helps make the change of key clear.

- Does the melody have a clear, recognisable line? ✓
- Does the melody move in steps with occasional leaps? ✓
- Is there a combination of similar and contrary motion between the melody and bass lines? ✓

Step 3 Modulating Prinner

In order to create more interest and to keep the momentum going, we further developed the rhythm in the melody line:

- Does the melody have some rhythmic variety to keep it interesting? ✓

It is quite common to find two Prinners in a row, the first remaining in the tonic, and the second modulating to the dominant key. This process adds motion and variety to the music and helps to create longer pieces of music as after moving away from the home key, there is a need to return there.

In the first movement of Mozart's *Violin Concerto No.3*, Mozart uses a tonic Prinner followed immediately by a dominant Prinner. Listen out for the continuation of the descent in the bass line. The dominant version increases the rate of harmonic change to generate energy towards the modulation.

TASK

1. Start to play around with the Prinner outline, experimenting with ways to develop it.

   a. If you are in $\frac{2}{4}$, you might like to double or halve the length or keep it the same.

   b. If you are in $\frac{3}{4}$, you may want to try two events per bar (minim followed by crotchet, for example), or one event per bar, using beats 2 and 3 to embellish the main note by leaping to other notes in the chord, or by connecting notes with scales.

   c. Keep the notes the same but change the rhythm.

   d. Leap to other notes in the same chord at each stage.

2. Start your Prinner on ❻ and ④ in the dominant key, allowing you to create a modulating Prinner that ends in the new key.

Musical references:
Mozart, W. A.: *Violin Concerto No.3 in G*, K.216 (i), bars 138–147 [Robert Levin / Renaud Capuçon / Orchestre de Chambre de Lausanne 4:23–4:41]

HOW TO CLOSE: CADENCE

Using schemata to start and continue a composition is an excellent way of composing quickly and stylishly. However, knowing how to punctuate your music is just as important if it is going to make sense. Music behaves like a language; it has a sense of order. In the same way that writing needs punctuation, we can use cadences to create points of arrival, pauses and 'full stops' in our musical phrases. We have already looked at how to begin a piece of music in the galant style using an opening schema, and we have learned about one way of responding to an initial idea – the Prinner. It is just as important to know how to complete a musical idea. At this stage we will add another point to our checklist for creating a good composition:

- **Is the structure clear and coherent, with convincing musical progression? ✓**

In the eighteenth century and to this day, this sense of structural cohesiveness is achieved using a cadence.

The perfect cadence

Let's begin with the strongest and most important type of cadence: the **perfect cadence**, also known as a **full close** or a **perfect authentic cadence**. There are four main features that make a perfect cadence. One is melodic, the second involves the bass line, the third is harmonic, and the fourth is rhythmical:

1. The melody moves step by step towards the tonic ❶. At a cadence, this often means the final movement is either ❼-❶ or ❷-❶. In many cases, the stepwise approach to the tonic happens over a longer span, with patterns such as ❸-❷-❶ and ❺-❹-❸-❷-❶ being very common.

2. The bass line always leaps from ⑤ to ①.

3. ⑤ supports a root-position dominant chord, or a root-position dominant 7th. ① supports a tonic chord in root position.

4. ⑤ is on a metrically weak part of the bar (for example, beat 2 of a $\frac{2}{4}$ bar). ① is on a metrically strong part of the bar (usually beat 1 in any time signature).

Common perfect cadence formulations

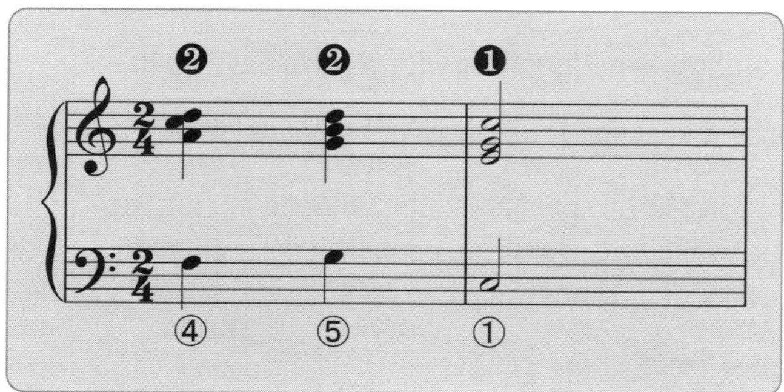

Descending onto the tonic from above is a very common melodic shape.

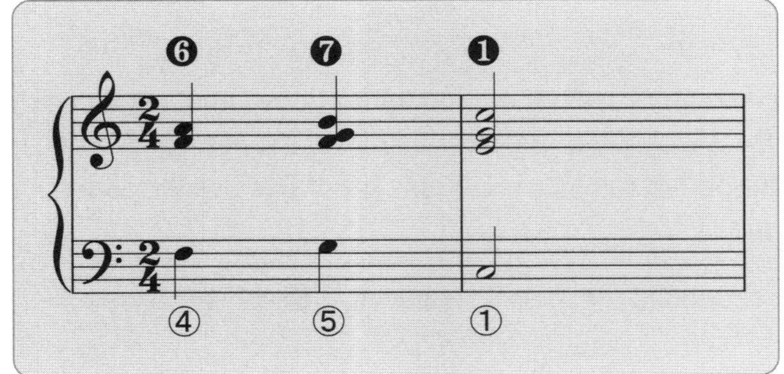

Ascending to the tonic from below creates a good sense of finality.

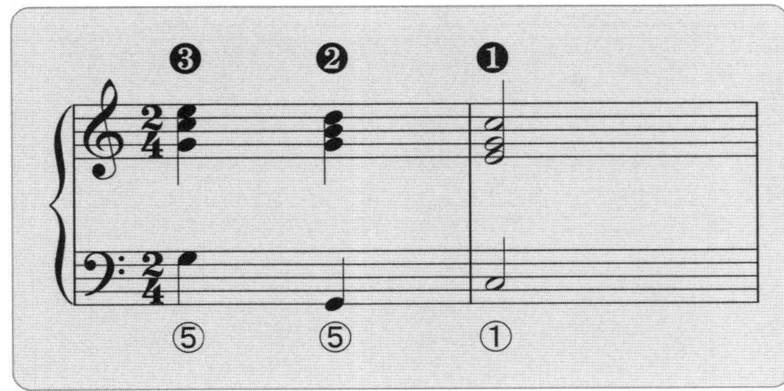

Contrary motion movement towards the tonic: The first chord here is in second inversion. The two highest voices must fall by step onto the next beat to make a root-position chord of G major before resolving to C major.

The next question is how to get to ⑤ in the bass. A bass line that ascends towards ⑤ is particularly effective and can be done in various ways. Cadential bass lines starting on ③ were very common, where ③ would usually be harmonised as a first inversion (6/3) chord. ④ offers a few possibilities: root position, first inversion, or a **secondary 7th** (in '6/5/3' position) are all common in the style.

Perfect cadence formulations with approaches to the dominant

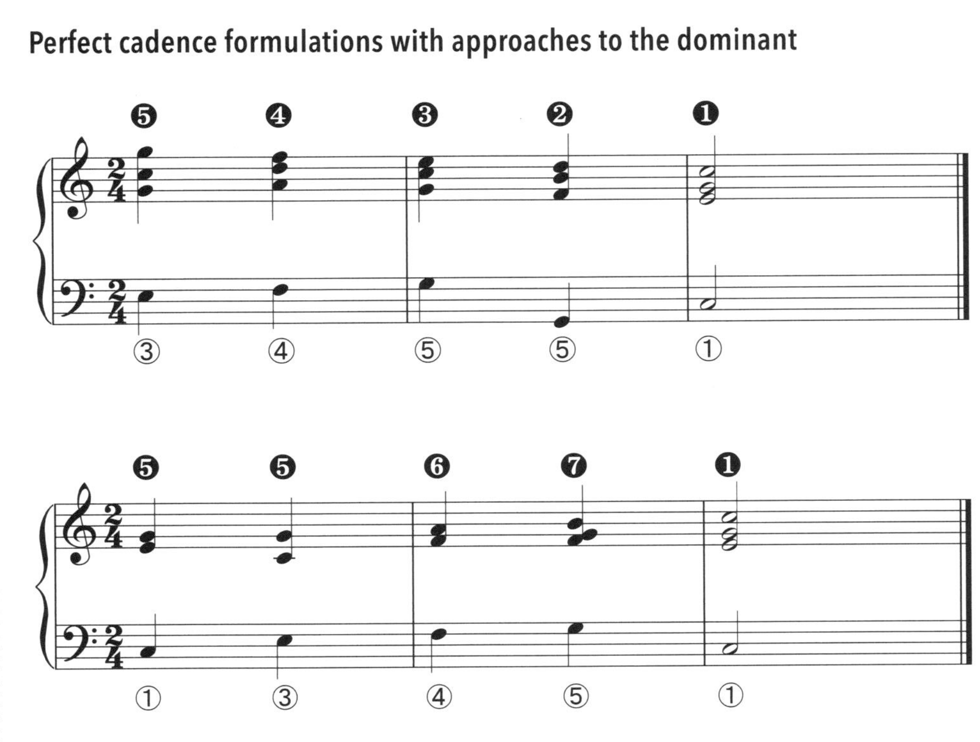

TOOLKIT: A WORKING EXAMPLE ✎

In our example so far, we have an opening Romanesca, a responding tonic Prinner, and a modulating Prinner. Our modulating Prinner currently ends with a G in the bass (the root of the new key) and a B in the melody. We now need to close this with a perfect cadence in the new key of G major, the dominant. So, our list of ways to create a perfect cadence is:

- Melody progressing towards ❶ – we continued the melody, following a ❸-❷-❶ shape to resolve on a G in the following bar.

- Bass line leaping from ⑤ to ①:

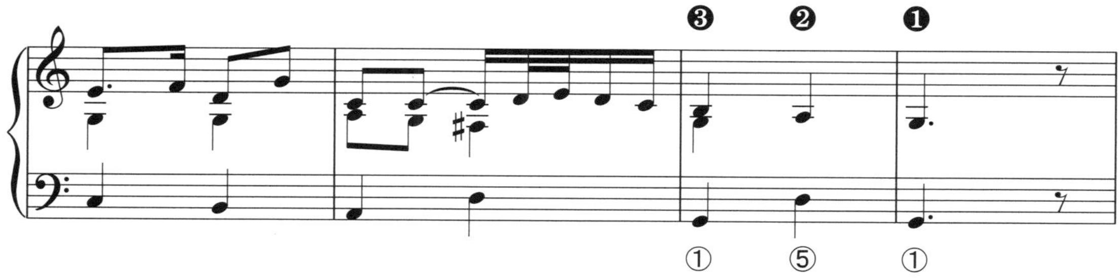

- ⑤ supports a root-position dominant chord, or a root-position dominant 7th. ① supports a tonic chord in root position. We added the F# above chord ⑤, which was missing its 3rd. This gives a really strong signal that the music has moved to a new key. We left ① without harmony notes, but implying a root-position chord:

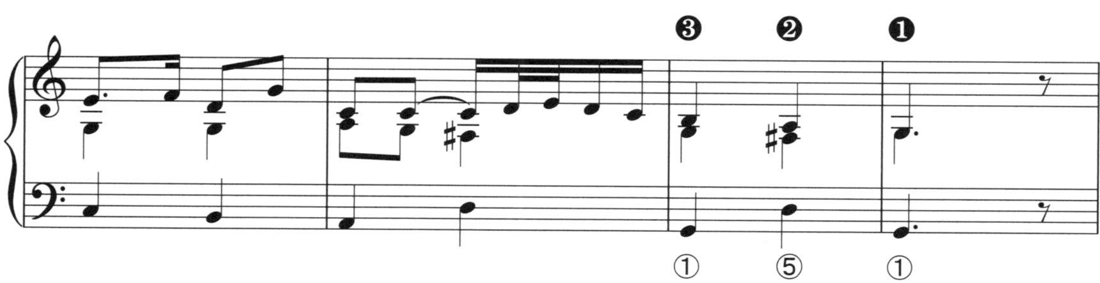

- ⑤ is on a weak part of the bar (beat 2). ① is on a strong part of the bar (beat 1).

Our next job was to tackle reaching ⑤ in the bass in a more interesting way. We decided to go with the ④-⑤-① shape, changing our crotchets to quavers to facilitate this. This automatically felt more energetic so we changed the rhythm in the melody to match this pace, adding in triplets for interest:

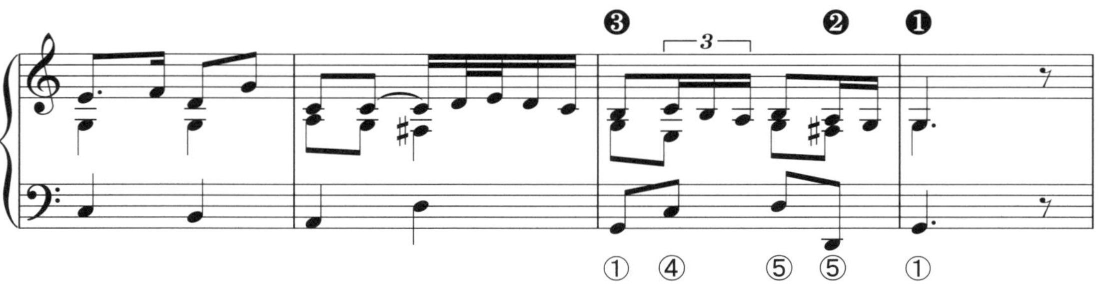

- Is the structure clear and coherent, with convincing musical progression? ✓

TASK

1. Play the different perfect cadence formulations outlined on pages 26–27 and decide on a version you like the sound of.

2. Start to work this into your existing Romanesca-Prinner sketch, making sure you:

   - Extend your Prinner melody so that it moves towards the tonic.

   - Support the cadence with ⑤-① bass motion.

   - Place ① on the downbeat of the final bar.

   - If necessary, adjust the rhythm in the melody to match the quicker rhythm in the bass.

Here is another cadence you may like to try:

The Cudworth cadence

Contrary motion (in which the melody and the bass move in opposite directions) is effective throughout a composition, but this works especially well in the approach to a cadence. In many galant-style cadences the bass often ascends toward ⑤, and a corresponding melodic descent to ❶ creates a balanced and elegant arrival. While a descent from ❸ or ❺ would be quite common, a full octave descent from high ❶ was a particular favourite in the mid-eighteenth-century style. The **Cudworth cadence** involves the same sort of bass line as above, but the melody runs down through the scale before slowing down at ❸ for the appoggiatura. The Cudworth cadence is very strong, and it is usually reserved only for important structural cadences at the end of a long passage of music, or to finish a whole piece.

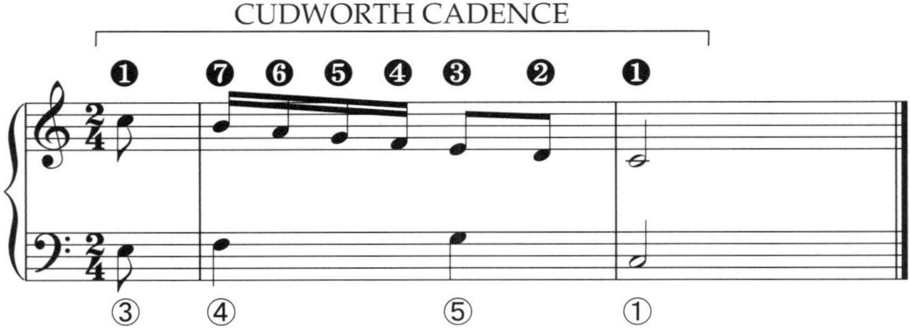

The galant-style double appoggiatura decorating a perfect cadence

One of the most common and stylish ways to decorate a cadence in the galant style was with the **double appoggiatura**. This way of decorating ⑤ was so widespread in the eighteenth century that it became the default option in the Classical style. If you're writing in a Classical style, once you have written your basic perfect cadence with ⑤ on the weak part of the bar, try extending your ⑤ back by a further beat (or, to put it slightly differently, arrive on ⑤ on a strong part of the bar: beat 3 in $\frac{4}{4}$ or beat 1 in $\frac{2}{4}$, for example). Above your ⑤ you can now write appoggiaturas (an upper-note decoration) that resolve onto your existing ❼ and ❷. This produces the melodic shapes ❸-❷ and ❶-❼.

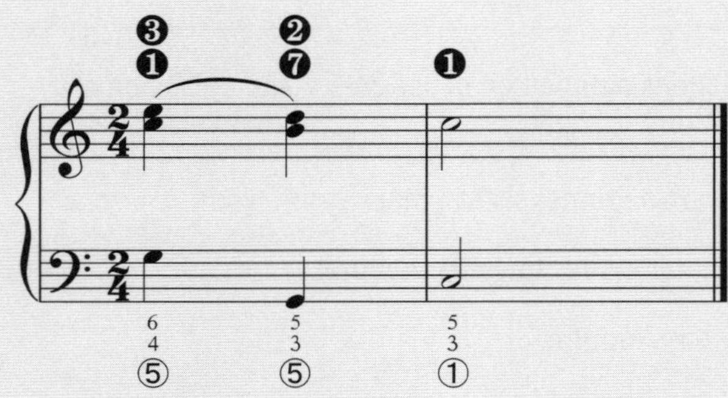

The appoggiatura will be treated as a dissonance which resolves downward by step to a consonant root-position chord. It is very common in eighteenth-century music to find composers doing this with two voices simultaneously – two appoggiaturas at the same time. This means that the bass stays on ⑤ for a moment longer to allow the double appoggiatura to resolve.

Double appoggiatura decorating a Cudworth cadence

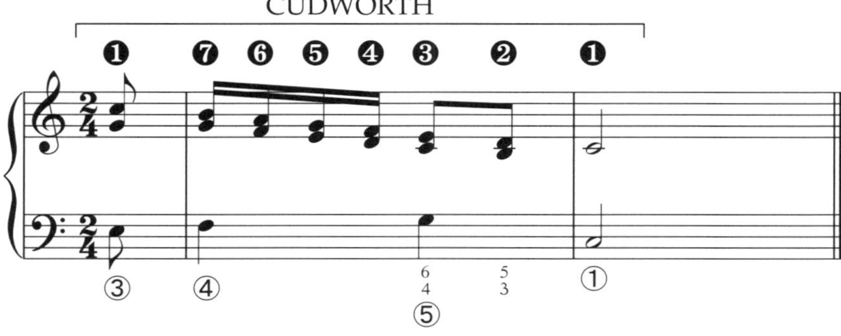

Prinner leading to a perfect cadence

There are different ways of using the Prinner to make a perfect cadence. The type of Prinner discussed above, in which the bass leaps to ⑤ before moving to ①, already somewhat resembles a perfect cadence. The problem is that the melody still only reaches ❸ in this formula – not the strongest indicator of closure.

The strongest way of ending a musical idea is to progress all the way to ❶ in the melody, and the most straightforward way to do this is to construct a Prinner and simply allow the melody to continue descending by adding ❷-❶ onto the end. This could be supported with a straightforward bass line:

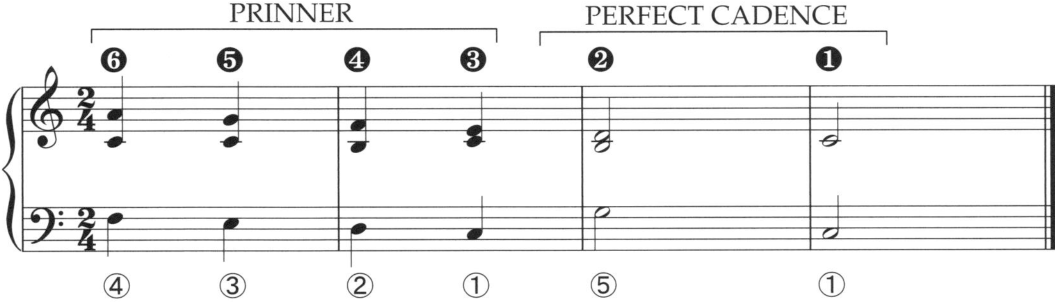

It could also be embellished with a suspension.

What is a suspension?

A suspension happens when a note from one chord is held over into the next chord, creating a brief clash (known as a **dissonance**) before it resolves. In the Prinner example below, the suspension happens in the first chord of the third bar, as the music approaches the perfect cadence:

- The C in the inner voice, made consonant by ①, becomes dissonant when it is held over the barline. It doesn't belong to the harmony of chord ⑤, so it now makes a dissonant 4th above ⑤.

- The dissonance needs to resolve by moving down by one step so that it makes a consonant 3rd above ⑤ in the bass.

You can add further weight to the cadence by inserting a predominant harmony – one that leads into ⑤ – using ④.

Prinner leading to a perfect cadence with decorative suspension

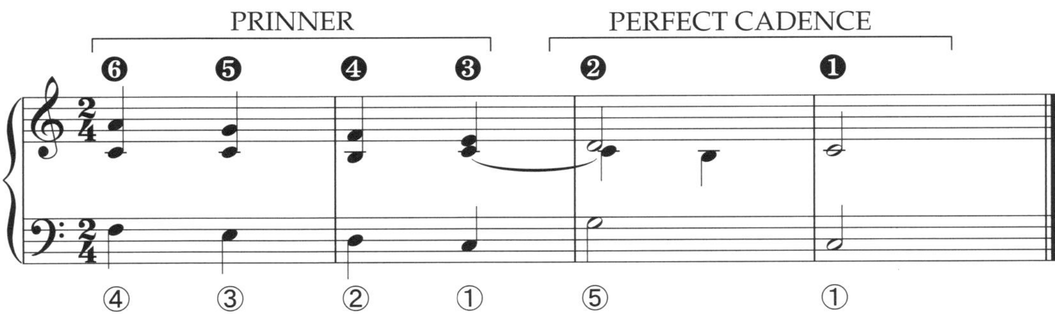

Prinner leading to a perfect cadence with decorative suspension and a predominant

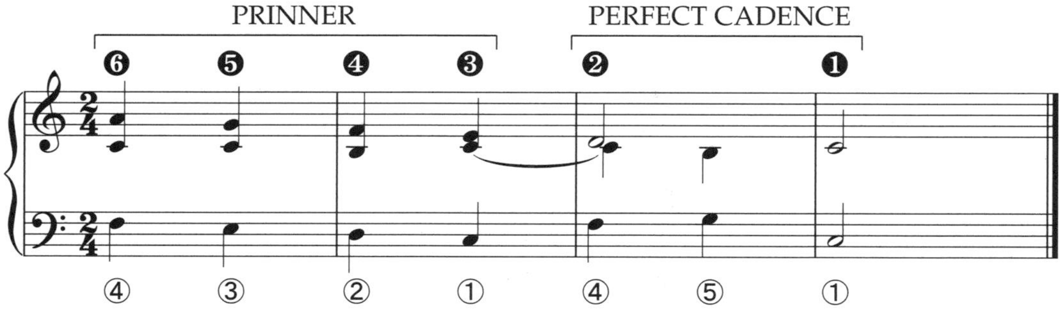

Notice in each of the examples that the basic rhythmic and harmonic principles are always observed: the cadence always lands on a strong beat, and the chords on ⑤ and ① are always in root position.

Prinner leading to an imperfect cadence

The basic shape of the Prinner's melodic voice is **❻-❺-❹-❸**. In order to produce an **imperfect cadence**, the melody needs to fall by one more step, down to **❷**. Likewise, the bass descent is ④-③-②-①. This means that the bass can leap to ⑤ from this point to achieve an imperfect cadence.

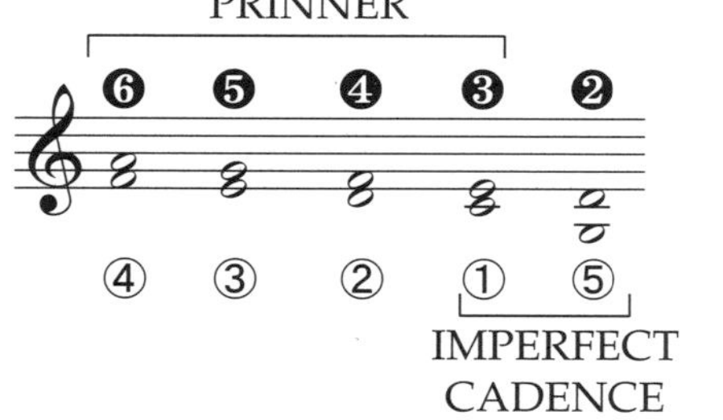

Listen to Sabrina Carpenter's *Please Please Please* [1:03–1:10] for a pop example of a Prinner approaching an imperfect cadence.

The imperfect cadence (or half close)

It was very common in galant music to stage a musical idea through the use of strategically positioned cadences – the perfect cadence was always positioned at the end of a complete musical idea. It is important, though, to set up some staging posts along the way. These are usually weaker cadences – something that signals a point of arrival but falls short of full closure. The most common of these is the **imperfect cadence** (half close or half cadence). The main characteristics of an imperfect cadence are:

1. The bass line stops on ⑤. This is what results in a 'half-finished' effect, with the implication that something has to come afterwards.

2. ⑤ supports a root-position dominant chord.

3. ⑤ is on a metrically strong part of the bar (usually beat 1 in any time signature).

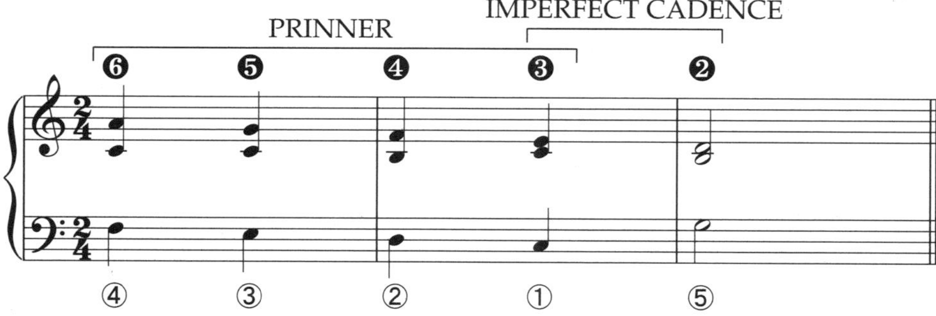

Once we have our opening Romanesca, responding tonic Prinner, and modulating Prinner, and we have closed with a perfect cadence, we have what we might call an 'A section':

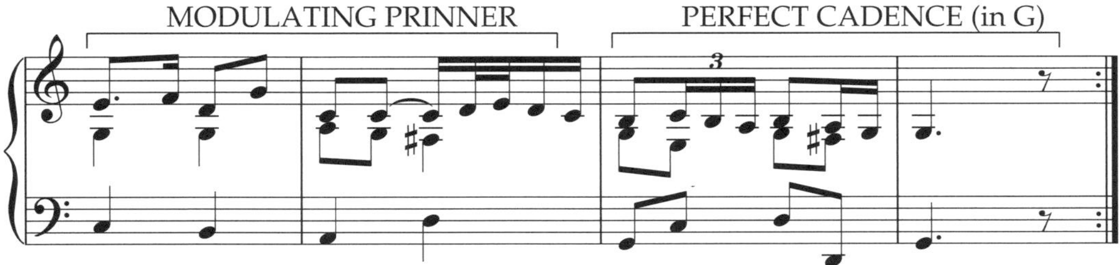

Let's consider our checklist to see if we could call this a good composition:

- **Does the melody have a clear, recognisable line?** ✓

    It is easy to pick the melody out of the texture.

- **Does the melody move in steps with occasional leaps?** ✓

    We have kept the melody mostly conjunct (moving in steps) with the odd leap to avoid it sounding static.

- **Does the melody have some rhythmic variety to keep it interesting?** ✓

    We've used some quite intricate rhythms such as demisemiquavers and triplets, but this isn't essential! You could stick to just crotchets, quavers, and some dotted rhythms to start off with.

- **Is there a clear bass line that underpins the melody?** ✓

    Using schemata achieves this immediately.

- **Is there a combination of similar and contrary motion between the melody and bass lines?** ✓

    Using schemata achieves this immediately.

- **Is there a clear sense of implied harmony?** ✓

    While using schemata strongly suggests the harmony, we've actually gone a step further throughout this part of the process and added some harmony notes. This was possible precisely because the harmony was so strongly implied by the shape of each schema.

- **Is the structure clear and coherent, with convincing musical progression?** ✓

    While this section is certainly coherent, we now need some more material to expand it into a full piece.

CONTRASTING SCHEMA: THE FONTE

Now we have two schemata to hand. We have the **Romanesca**, which is good for starting a piece of music, and the **Prinner**, which is good for responding to the Romanesca as well as moving from one key to the next. While these schemata are very versatile, it is necessary to add some contrast and variety. We need something to help us to achieve the next step we're adding to our composition checklist:

- Does the piece have some contrasting material?

The **Fonte** schema is good for this because it involves a mixture of major and minor elements. 'Fonte' is an Italian word meaning 'font' or 'well'. The schema was given this name because it invokes the action of sinking, owing to its downward sequential motion. The main features of the Fonte schema are:

- It happens in two stages
- Stage one is minor, stage two is major
- Stage two is a step lower than stage one

In eighteenth-century music the most common place to find the Fonte schema is immediately after a double barline in the middle of a piece of music. This is usually the place where composers want to generate a sense of contrast. The Fonte achieves this very effectively not only because it temporarily treats a new key as the tonic, but especially because that new key is minor instead of major. It is also a useful way of leading back home to the tonic.

In its most basic form, each stage of the Fonte consists of motion from dominant to tonic. This can be in root position, resulting in a bass line that moves from ⑤ to ①, or the more stylish version that involves a first-inversion dominant moving to a root-position tonic (⑦ to ①). The bass line usually supports the ❹ to ❸ descent in the melody, establishing effective contrary-motion movement. If that takes care of the internal events of each stage, how does the whole Fonte work?

Fonte with ⑤-① bass

Fonte with ⑦-① bass

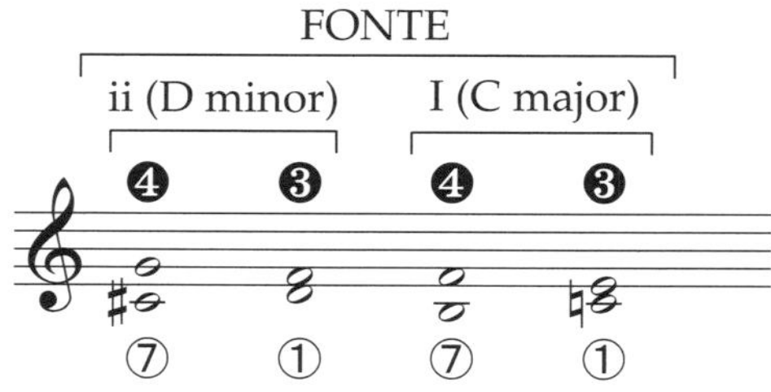

This is a very flexible schema with many options, but the most common is to descend from stage one in the supertonic minor (ii) to stage two in the tonic major (I).

In both cases the Fonte can simply begin its passage from outlining chord ii and it will always lead back to the tonic. Similar to the Prinner, it can also be embellished and stretched out over longer spans as needed.

Stamitz: *Symphony in F major*

The Fonte in popular music

While less common in contemporary genres, the Fonte occasionally appears in popular music.

 In the 80s synth-pop song *It's My Life* by Talk Talk, a Fonte kicks off the pre-chorus before the vocals come in [0:49–1:20]. The Fonte then continues to provide the shape for the chorus.

In both contrasting examples from Stamitz and Talk Talk the effect of using a Fonte is that the tension is built by moving away from the tonic, before being released through the return to it. This technique can be used in many styles of music where the aim is to create some harmonic variety.

TOOLKIT: A WORKING EXAMPLE

Step 1 Fonte outline

For our example, we mapped out the outline of a Fonte, opting for the ⑦ to ① bass in both stages:

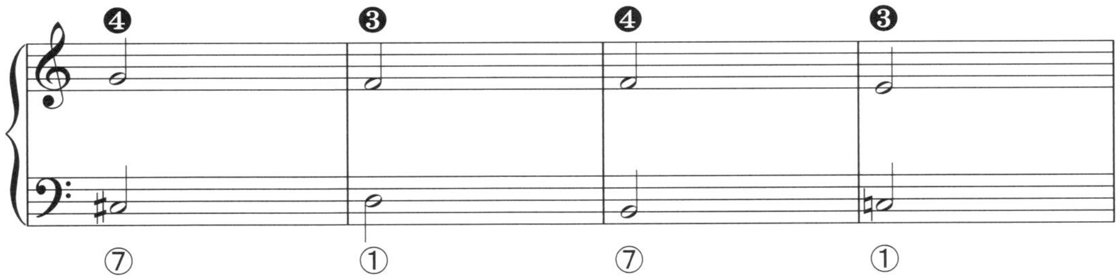

- Is there a clear bass line that underpins the melody? ✓
- Is there a combination of similar and contrary motion between the melody and bass lines? ✓
- Is there a clear sense of implied harmony? ✓
- Does the piece have some contrasting material? ✓

Step 2 Fonte + harmony

We then added some harmony notes in an inner voice, helping to thicken the texture:

- The first two chords are both A major triads in different inversions. The 5th is missing from both, so we added the E to the inner voice.
- The D minor harmony in the second bar could be filled out with either an A or another D. We decided to choose D in order to prevent the inner voice from leaping around too much.

Musical references:
Stamitz, Johann: *Symphony in F major*, Op.4, No.1, iii, bars 9–12

- The third bar is similar to bar 1. Both chords are expressions of G major, but the D is missing, so we added it to the inner voice.

- Bar 4 is similar to bar 2 – it follows the same pattern but down a step, so we moved the inner voice down to the C.

We matched this momentum by turning the bass line minims into crotchets, adding extra notes where necessary to outline the harmony:

- Does the melody move in steps with occasional leaps? ✓

Step 3 Fonte

We were then able to improvise around this outline, eventually landing on another dotted rhythm to match the rhythm of our original Romanesca:

- Does the melody have a clear, recognisable line? ✓
- Does the melody have some rhythmic variety to keep it interesting? ✓

Closing your sketch

Now that the Fonte has brought the music back to the tonic, the last thing to do is to close the piece in that key. Although a perfect cadence on its own might do the job, it is more musically satisfying to reuse some of the music that we heard in the first half of the piece first. The two options are either to start again using the Romanesca, or use the Prinner as an approach to a perfect cadence. We opted for the second strategy using the Prinner idea originally heard in bar 5. Because we have revisited the material from our A section, we call this **rounded binary form**. It is important to note that this Prinner must lead to the tonic, not the dominant. We begin on F in the bass (④) and allow it to move to a final cadence in the tonic key. Since this cadence is also the end of the whole piece, we decided to embellish it by starting higher up the scale and creating a longer descent down to the final tonic – an example of a **Cudworth Cadence** (see page 29). Typically, both sections in binary form are repeated, so all that remains now is to add the repeat marks:

Complete rounded binary form using Romanesca, Prinner, and Fonte

Once you have a **Romanesca**, **Prinner**, **modulating Prinner**, and a **Fonte**, and have decided a way to close your ideas with a cadence, you have the ingredients of a basic structure. If you have followed the steps of **Part I**, you should have a binary form piece – that is, a balanced piece in two sections where section A begins in the tonic and ends in the dominant, and section B (after the double bar) contains tonal contrast and ends in the tonic.

Take a look at **Parts II** and **III** to explore how to develop these materials and expand this piece into a larger-scale composition.

PART II: MUSICAL FORM

Now that we have a set of musical ideas that we can use to build a composition, let's look at some of the established ways of ordering them so that we can fulfil the requirements of our newest point on our checklist: **Is the structure clear and coherent, with convincing musical progression?** In this section we will explore different schematic pathways – ways of combining schemata to create a larger musical form. These details help give music its shape and sense of direction.

In a sense, composing a piece of music is like writing a story. It needs to have a beginning, a middle and an end, and this has the effect of making the music sound like it has direction and purpose.

ARRANGING SCHEMATA INTO A MUSICAL FORM

In **Part I** we saw how it is possible, using just three schemata, to build a piece of music with a beginning, a middle and an end. The piece we have created is in **rounded binary form**, which is one of the simplest ways to structure music. It is the basis of the most common forms found in the Classical repertoire, which include the minuet and trio, variation form, and rondo form.

How it works

Rounded binary form is divided into two parts that are usually identified by double barlines with repeat marks. It follows this basic pattern:

- Opening section (a) – presents the main idea of the piece, usually moves away from the tonic and ends with a double barline.

- After the double barline (ba) – a new idea is presented, but before the end, 'a' returns, usually in a modified or shortened format.

Because the 'a' section returns before the end, (albeit often in a modified or shortened version) rounded binary can sound a bit like ternary form (ABA). However, the way the music moves through different keys still feels more like binary form because it happens in two separate motions, one that moves away from the tonic, and a second that returns to it.

There are several options for the music before the double barline:

- Remain in the same key, closing with a perfect cadence

- Leave it open-ended with an imperfect cadence

- Modulate to a new key (V if the piece is in the major mode, III if it's minor) and close with a perfect cadence in the new key.

In our worked example from **Part I**, we opted to modulate to the dominant – in this case, G major – and to close the 'a' section with a perfect cadence in the new key. After using a Fonte to generate new material for the 'b' section, we then repeated the Prinner from bars 3–4, embellishing the melody line slightly, before closing in the tonic key of C major.

Moving away from the tonic key is important in tonal music because it generates a sense of tension, just as a good story needs twists and turns to keep it exciting. Moving to the dominant key in the middle is the most straightforward way of creating a dynamic structure and giving your piece a sense of purpose. This rounded binary form is the most basic way of generating a musical structure. We will now learn about some of the other approaches that can lead to more substantial musical forms.

VARIATION FORM

Sets of variations on a theme were very common in the eighteenth century, and they are relatively straightforward to construct following Classical practice. Variations are most frequently based on a theme in rounded binary form (discussed above). Each new variation can become increasingly complicated through the use of shorter note values, more decorative scoring, additional layers of counterpoint, and sometimes a shift of mode (e.g. from major to minor).

Variation form in action

In this example by Somis we can see how the composer relies on ever shorter note values to turn a 1-minute piece into a 5-minute piece:

- The theme uses mainly crotchets and quavers

- Variation 1 uses quavers in the violin melody

- Variation 2 uses triplets

- Variation 3 uses semiquavers

- The original theme is heard again, providing balance and symmetry. The implication is that the violinist would add in their own decorations here.

The original theme is constructed using rounded binary form and uses only three schemata. The bass line (provided in the first example only) stays the same throughout. This is a clear example of the efficient use of musical materials that was commonplace in eighteenth-century composition.

Somis: *Minuet* from *Violin Sonata in C Major: Theme* (Violin melody with bass accompaniment)

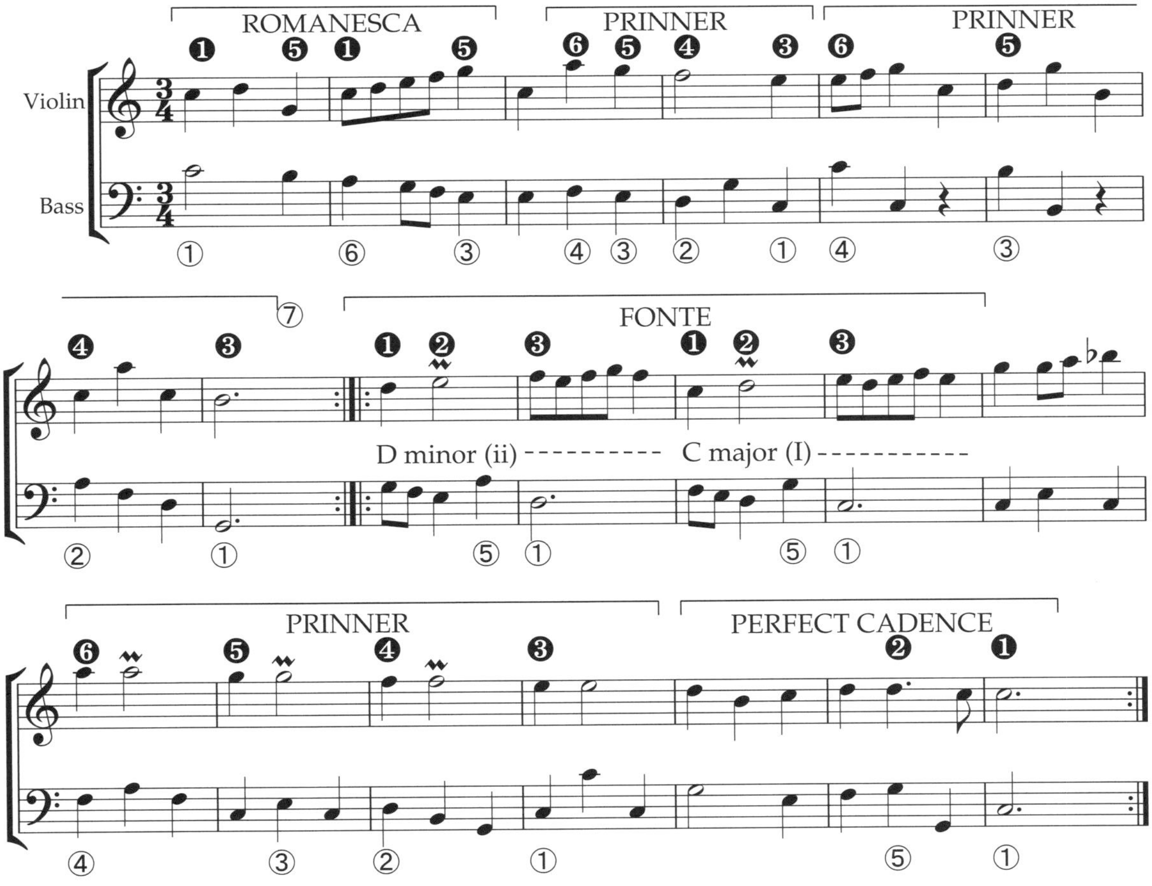

Musical references:
Somis, Giovanni Battista: *Minuet* from *Violin Sonata in C Major*, Op. 6, No. 4

Variation 1, bars 1–8 (Violin melody only)

Variation 2, bars 1–8 (Violin melody only)

Variation 3, bars 1–8 (Violin melody only)

TOOLKIT: A WORKING EXAMPLE

We can apply this strategy to the rounded binary piece from **Part I**. Using the original as a theme, we create three variations that keep the same 16-bar structure while adding more rhythmic embellishment each time. These are played in order, followed by a final return of the unvaried theme (with optional performer embellishment). The structure would look something like this:

Theme	Variation 1	Variation 2	Variation 3	Theme
In its original form, mainly quavers in the melody	Mainly semiquavers in the melody	Mainly triplets in the melody	Mainly demisemiquavers in the melody	In its original form

Theme

Variation 1

We have used the notes in the chord to guide the semiquaver melody. For example, the first beat of the first bar of the theme is a C major chord, so we have used the notes C, E, and G in the melody. This means we can remove the extra harmony notes we originally included in the theme, as the harmony is so clearly outlined by the much busier melody line.

Variation 2

As with Variation 1, we stuck to using notes from the chord to guide our semiquaver triplet melody.

Variation 3

We have used a mixture of scalic and arpeggio patterns to give us the combination of conjunct and disjunct movement we were looking for in our original checklist.

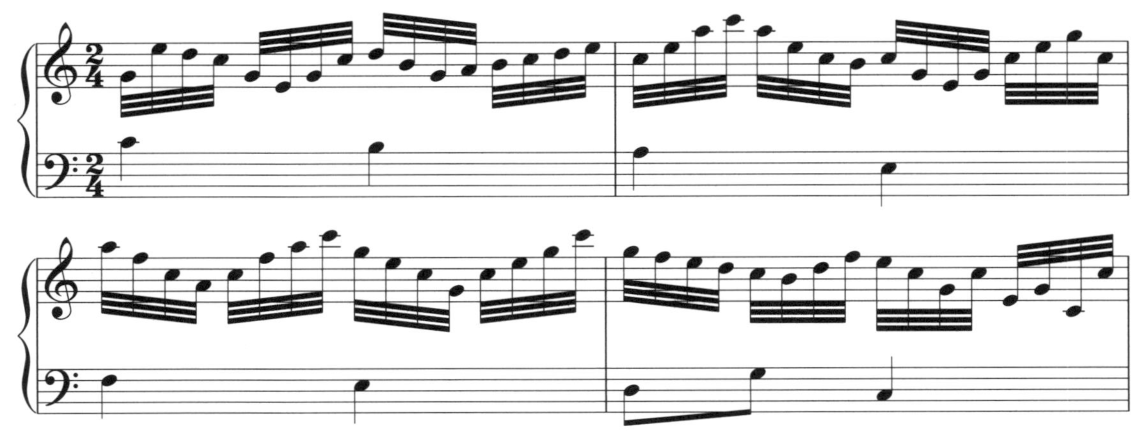

1. Complete each of the variations on p.41 using the openings provided. Keep the rhythm at the start of each variation going until the end and try to use either scales or arpeggios, or a mixture of both.

More advanced variation techniques also exist, and you might like to experiment with these or even combine them. Listen to the examples suggested below for even more inspiration.

- Changing from major to minor
- Changing time signature, perhaps from duple to triple metre (e.g. $\frac{2}{4}$ to $\frac{3}{4}$) or from simple to compound time (e.g. $\frac{2}{4}$ to $\frac{6}{8}$).
- Changing key by placing a variation in the subdominant, dominant, relative minor, or submediant.
- Embellishing the bass voice instead of the melody

2. Now experiment with changing the rhythm of the melody in your own initial idea, making the note lengths shorter each time. Try using one of the options from the list above as a way of further developing your material to create a theme and set of variations.

Theme and variations across styles

Fernando Sor – *Introduction and Variations on a Theme by Mozart*: Keeps variation principles transparent and easy to follow.

Edward Elgar – *Enigma Variations*: Strong example of character variation and orchestration.

Ernst von Dohnányi – *Variations on a Nursery Song*: Playful and ironic, clear in structure and easy to analyse.

Carl Nielsen – *Chaconne*: Excellent for exploring variation over ostinato patterns.

Charles Ives – *Variations on America*: Demonstrates variation through collage, distortion, and quotation.

George Gershwin – *Variations on I Got Rhythm*: Shows jazz-influenced harmonic variation and rhythmic transformation.

Federico Mompou – *Variations on a Theme by Chopin*: Illustrates economy, colour, and restraint rather than virtuosic display.

Sergei Rachmaninov – *Rhapsody on a Theme of Paganini*: Exemplifies a large-scale Romantic-to-modern variation arc.

William Walton – *Variations on a Theme by Hindemith*: Shows how textures and instrumental roles can be reshaped to create variation.

TERNARY FORM

Ternary form differs from binary form in that it creates contrast rather than maintaining one mood throughout the piece.

How it works

- An opening section – let's call it the **'A' section** – which opens and closes in the same key, ending with a perfect cadence. This can be organised as a rounded binary form, as above.

- A contrasting **'B' section** in a different key and with new thematic material. This can also be organised as a rounded binary form.

- A return of the **'A' section**, sometimes with some significant variation from the first A section.

Ternary form is therefore understood as being in three sections – **ABA** – in which the middle B section contrasts with the surrounding A sections in terms of key, mode, theme, dynamics, or even tempo in some cases.

The B section of a ternary form can vary in the way it is organised. However, the most straightforward way to do this is to write a completely new binary form. This can be done by using the basic shape laid out above, but with different schemata and in a related key. A binary form in the dominant, subdominant, relative, or tonic minor would all be possibilities in the eighteenth century.

Ternary form in popular music

AABA song structure, often referred to as 32-bar form, is a type of ternary form that is frequently used in folk and popular music. If you are composing for voice and accompaniment, and especially if you are composing in a non-classical style, this is a good structure to explore. In AABA form, each section lasts for 8 bars, with the material of the first 8-bar phrase repeating with different lyrics before the music moves to a contrasting B section, often called a bridge. The material from the A section then returns.

A good example of this can be heard *Over the Rainbow* by Yip Harburg with the opening melody ("Somewhere over the rainbow…") returning after a contrasting middle section, ("Someday I'll wish upon a star…").

It is also a popular song structure in jazz. The jazz standard *Blue Moon* (Rodgers/Hart) follows the same pattern as *Over the Rainbow*, with each verse starting with the same words before moving on to something different [starting at 0:16].

In The Cure's *Friday I'm In Love*, the recurring A sections feature the title hook at the end, demonstrating how repetition in form can be adapted in popular music.

We decided to keep the same basic binary structure for the B section of our composition. It would be too samey to use a Romanesca again, though, so we chose another schema for this passage: **the Meyer**.

OPENING SCHEMA: THE MEYER

This commonly used Classical schema functioned as an alternative to the Romanesca, and it has many variants that invite experimentation. It is better to think of the Meyer as a family of schemata rather than a single, fixed pattern. In its most basic and common form, the Meyer is a schema that unfolds in two stages:

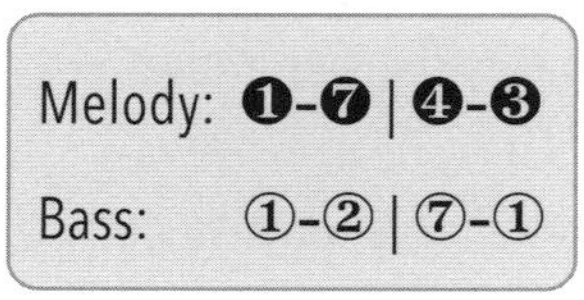

The Meyer in action

Though not at the start of a piece, this example by Schubert is probably one of the most straightforward examples of the Meyer schema you are likely to hear in the repertoire. The only addition to the basic shape in this case is the decorated inner pedal point on ❺, which propels the rhythmic profile of the movement even during this quieter and more reflective passage.

Schubert: *Quintet in A major, 'Trout'*

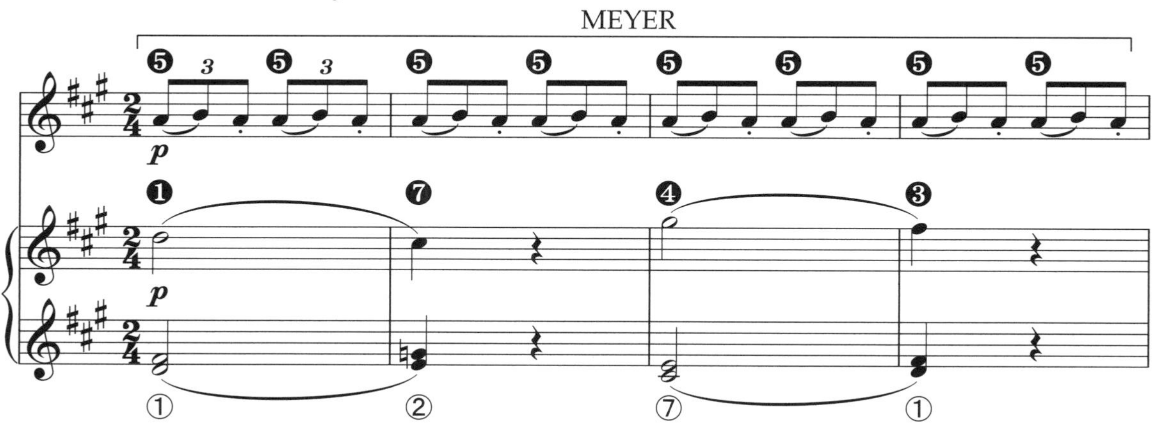

The next example, also by Schubert, is more typical: it appears at the start of a large form and is decorated. This decoration happens in three ways. First, the melody drops an octave before a rapid scalic rise, adding energy and momentum. Second, the arrival is decorated with an appoggiatura, creating a reassuring sense of arrival. Third, the gap between the two stages of the schema is filled by an interjection, echoed again at the end of the schema.

Schubert: *Symphony No.1 in D Major* (piano reduction)

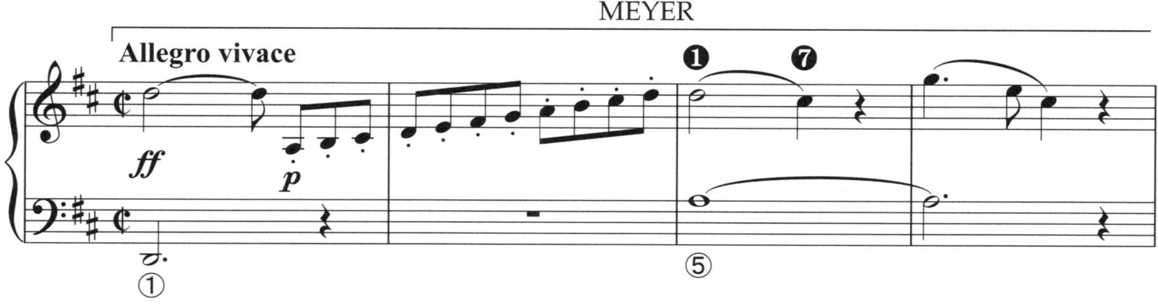

Musical references:
Schubert, Franz: *Quintet in A major, 'Trout'*, D.667, v, bars 195–198
Schubert, Franz: *Symphony No.1 in D Major*, D.82, bars 21–28

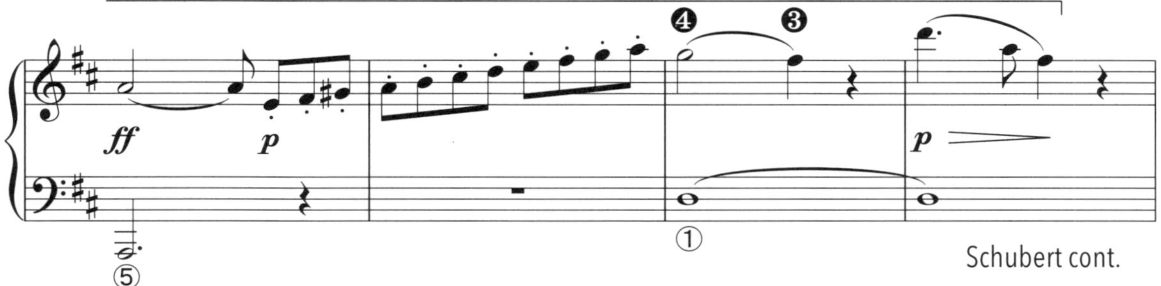

In this case, the interjections are played by the woodwind, adding a momentary change of colour. Schubert achieves this by arpeggiating the chord downwards (contrasting with the violins' upward scale) while ensuring the interjections do not interrupt the main schema. The two halves of the Meyer are also rhythmically and melodically balanced, sharing the same profile despite using different notes, reflecting the Classical ethos of balance and symmetry.

TOOLKIT: A WORKING EXAMPLE

In order to create contrast we set our B section in a related key, the subdominant (F major). Moving towards the 'flat side' like this has the effect of relaxing the tonal tension of the piece. Moving to the 'sharp side', to G major for example, has the opposite effect of increasing the tension. Our first step was to map out the Meyer schema in our new key:

Meyer outline

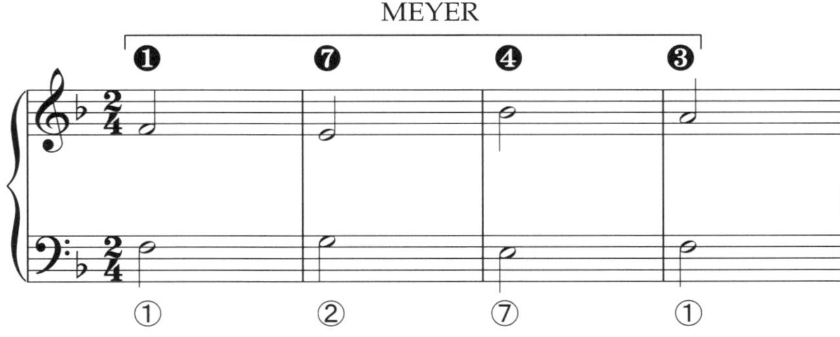

We kept this section simpler, in contrast to the more ornate A section. The main notes of the Meyer schema are undecorated, with additional harmony notes added to enrich the texture:

Meyer + harmony

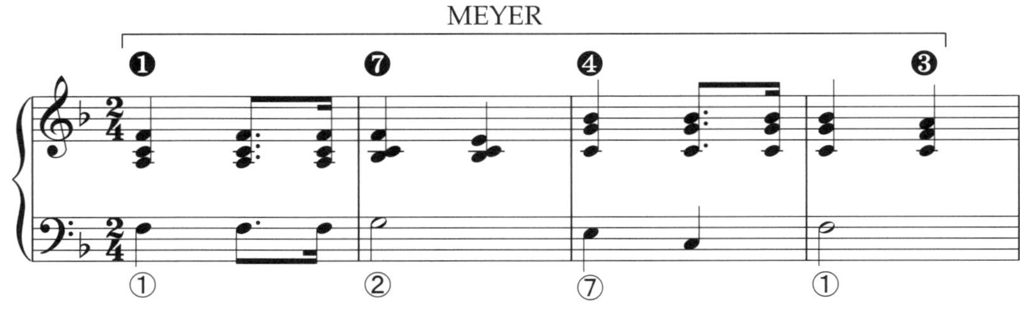

We then used a Prinner as a means of producing an imperfect cadence, landing on a chord of C major:

Meyer + Prinner

If we are aiming for another rounded binary section then this is a good point to insert a double barline. We now need some contrasting material to start the next section, so we opted to return to the Fonte. Notice how the rhythm of the Fonte is the same as the Meyer that we started with. This helps to create a sense of internal coherence (in which the crotchet rest at the end of every two bars is a feature) and forward motion towards the cadence as the note values become shorter and the rests disappear. After the Fonte takes the music back to F major, we simply rounded off the binary structure with a Prinner and a perfect cadence, followed by repeat marks. The B section might seem quite plain when viewed in isolation, but its aim is to generate contrast with the A section, and not to stand on its own.

B section in F major using the Meyer, Prinner and Fonte

See **Appendix 1** for our full ternary form worked example. Our original rounded binary form piece from **Part I** is used as the A section and our new rounded binary form from above is the B section. Instead of writing out the A section again for the return, we have used *Da capo al fine* markings.

TASK

Try organising your ideas into a ternary form piece. Instead of beginning your B section with another Romanesca, try using an alternative such as a **Meyer** or a **Do-Re-Mi** (see **Rondo Form** on page 50) and then follow the pathway to the dominant and back again.

MINUET AND TRIO FORM

The **minuet and trio** is a common form found in large-scale works of the eighteenth century. It consists of two rounded binary structures – the minuet and the trio. These can be composed independently of each other, though it is a good idea to think about how they might create contrast through theme, key, mode, and texture.

How it works

- The opening minuet is organised in rounded binary form.
- This is followed by the trio, which uses contrasting thematic material but is still in rounded binary form.
- The minuet is then repeated (often through the use of *Da Capo al Fine*).

This kind of departure-and-return design isn't unique to Classical dance forms. The same expressive curve shapes film cues and songs that build to a reprise – a return that feels both familiar and renewed.

The minuet and trio in 20th century music

Maurice Ravel – *Menuet antique*: A modern take on the minuet form that combines Classical dance structure with Ravel's characteristic harmonic colour and subtle rhythmic flexibility.

Igor Stravinsky's *Pulcinella Minuets* demonstrate Neoclassical transformation of minuet style. Baroque dance forms are reimagined through 20th-century harmonic and rhythmic language.

Dmitri Shostakovich – *Symphony No. 5, Second Movement*: The minuet and trio feel is embedded in a symphonic scherzo combining Classical dance forms with expressive, 20th-century harmonic language.

Minuet and trio form in action

This is shown clearly in Mozart's *Eine Kleine Nachtmusik* below. The minuet ends in the home key of G major then the trio brings in contrasting material in the dominant key of D major.

Mozart: *Minuet and trio* from *Eine Kleine Nachtmusik* (piano reduction)

Musical references:
Mozart, W. A: *Minuet and trio* from *Eine Kleine Nachtmusik*, K.525

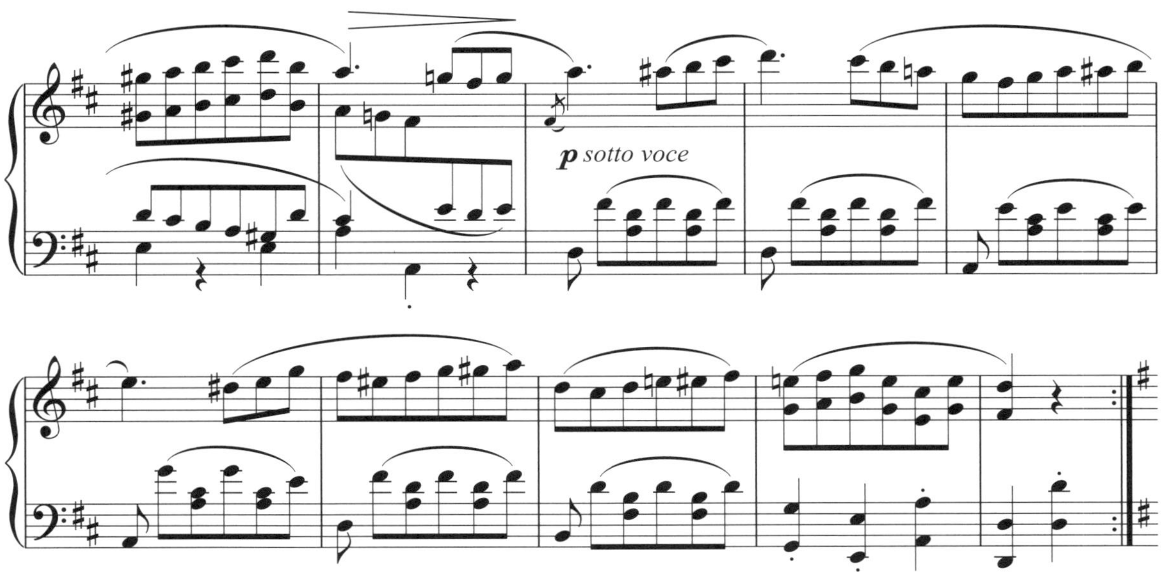

A minuet has to be in triple metre (nearly always $\frac{3}{4}$). This is a defining metrical feature and part of its identity as a stately dance – if it doesn't have 3 beats in each bar then it's not a minuet! As our original example was written in $\frac{2}{4}$, we decided to convert the same material into $\frac{3}{4}$ time to create a minuet and trio.

TOOLKIT: A WORKING EXAMPLE

Here are the first 8 bars of what is now our minuet section. Notice how we kept the chord changes on the third beat of the bar:

Theme recomposed as a minuet in $\frac{3}{4}$

You can find our full minuet and trio worked example, (which is a $\frac{3}{4}$ version of our ternary form example), in **Appendix 1**. Instead of writing out the minuet again for the return, we have used the Italian instruction *Da Capo al Fine*.

1. Convert the rest of your original rounded binary form into a $\frac{3}{4}$ minuet and trio form.

2. Now take your initial idea from **Part I** and convert it into a minuet making sure it's in $\frac{3}{4}$. Then create a new rounded binary section to become the trio. Often, trio sections are more lyrical and relaxed. A good way to achieve this is to go to the subdominant key (IV). If you already created a ternary form piece, you could convert the whole thing into a minuet and trio by rewriting it in $\frac{3}{4}$ time!

TOP TIP

If you are composing exam coursework, it is better to avoid using **Da Capo al Fine** *as this can compromise your ability to demonstrate development of ideas. Instead, write out the minuet again but use some of the ideas from* **Part III** *to elaborate the material.*

RONDO FORM

It is rare to find a **rondo** anywhere other than in the last movement of a multi-movement work (e.g. a string quartet, piano sonata or symphony). It is one of the easiest forms to understand and it was often found in the light, frothy final movement rather than the more serious first and second movements.

How it works

- Main theme (A) – usually light in character and easily recognisable
- Contrasting episode (B) – change of theme and key
- Return of A in the tonic key
- Contrasting episode (C) – change of theme and key
- Return of A in the tonic

The main theme of a rondo is usually set in rounded binary form with the theme neatly closed in its own key. It also contains quite a lot of repetition, making subsequent returns of the theme easy for the audience to recognise and anticipate.

The A section is in the tonic key each time, whereas the contrasting episodes (B, C, etc.) feature a change of theme and key which adds variety to the music while also delaying the next repetition of the theme. The episodes themselves were often composed in short binary forms, creating enough contrast in each episode to keep the dynamism of the music going without making them so different that the music loses its sense of direction. The structure of a rondo movement can be understood as ABACA, or sometimes ABACBA.

Rondo form in Romantic and 20th century music

Gustav Mahler – Finale, *Symphony No. 7*: A driving main theme, fanfare-like brass, and contrasting dark episodes.

Camille Saint-Saëns – *Introduction and Rondo Capriccioso*: A lively rondo with virtuosic solo passages contrasting with the recurring theme.

Leonard Bernstein – *Rondo for Lifey*: A modern rondo featuring jazz-inflected episodes.

Benjamin Britten – *Introduction and Rondo alla Burlesca*, Op. 23, No. 1: A witty rondo where the theme returns varied through rhythmic and harmonic shifts.

Choosing a schema

Creating a rondo is straightforward if you have already followed the steps to make a ternary form. This is because the rondo can be seen as an extension of ternary form in which ABA becomes ABACA. Therefore, we will need yet another binary form for our C section that contrasts with both A (in the tonic) and B (in the subdominant). We will also need to choose a different opening schema so that the music doesn't become too repetitive. In our case, we chose for our C section to be in A minor (the relative minor of C major), and we began with the **Do-Re-Mi** schema.

THE DO-RE-MI

This is one of the simplest schemata. As the name suggests, the melody ascends: **❶-❷-❸**. This can be supported with a number of bass lines. The two most common are ①-⑦-① and ①-⑤-①. The drawback of this simplicity is that the schema can be over in a flash if it is left in its undecorated state, so composers found interesting, witty, and ingenious ways of stretching this schema out over a longer span.

The Do-Re-Mi in action

This example by Mozart is a relatively plain use of the Do-Re-Mi. Here the main thing that is expanding each stage of the schema is the rhythm, which hardly changes note as it proceeds. You will notice, however, that the first event (① supporting ❶) is decorated harmonically. The melody seems temporarily to step either side of the core note, and is supported by ⑤ in the bass, before returning to the core tones of the schema. Likewise, when Mozart progresses to the second event (⑤ supporting ❷) he decorates ⑤ with tonic harmony before returning to the core tones of the schema. This is a very common treatment of the Do-Re-Mi, and it is not a harmonically complex one. Mozart only uses chords I and V of the home key.

Mozart: *Piano Concerto No. 18*

TOOLKIT: A WORKING EXAMPLE

After starting our C section with a **Do-Re-Mi** schema, we followed it with a **modulating Prinner**. The end of the Do-Re-Mi (landing on A in the bass and C in the melody) becomes the beginning of the Prinner in the dominant key: E minor. In the eighteenth century this was the second most common destination from a minor key starting point; the most common choice was to move to the relative major (which would have been C major). However, in this piece there has already been a lot of major-key activity so we decided to keep the music in the minor mode and visit a key we haven't seen yet. We followed the tried-and-tested pathway to return to A minor after the double bar: **Fonte – Prinner – cadence**. The last thing to do at this point – an optional extra – is to soften the return to C major for the concluding A section by adding a **transitional chord** of G major to link the two sections. G major belongs to both keys of E minor (the 'old' key) and C major (the key the music is moving to). It is also the dominant of C major, which is the most efficient way to return to that tonal area.

'C section' of a rondo

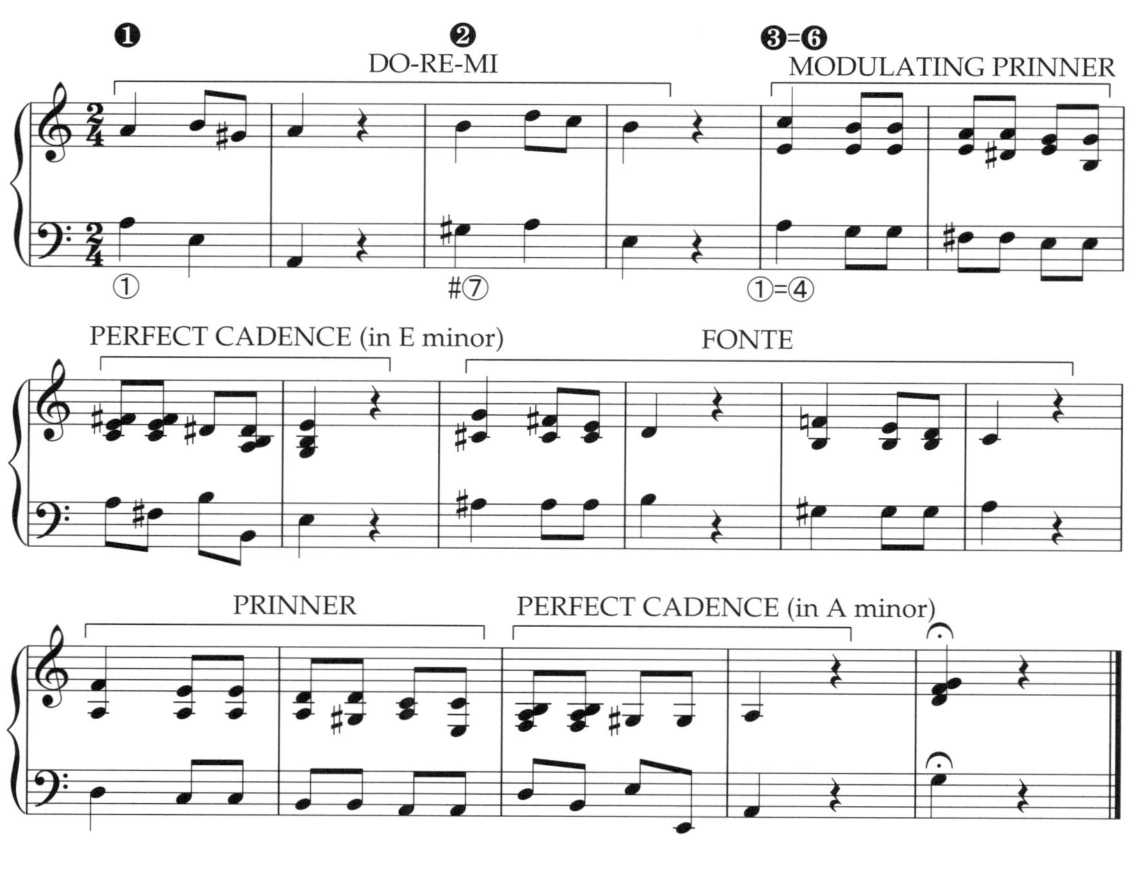

Musical references:

Williams, John: *Binary Sunset (The Force Theme)* from *Star Wars: A New Hope* [0:07–0:12]

In this rondo we hear the A section 3 times and it is in the same key of C major each time we hear it. Composers would sometimes vary the repetitions of the rondo theme (the A section) each time it returned. This process results in the structure ABA'CA''. If you have already followed the above steps to make a series of variations on your original theme then you could always use these variations in place of the theme for the rondo returns. That way there will be enough similarity for the listener to recognise that the theme has returned, but enough variety to avoid sounding repetitious. You can find our full rondo worked example with this new C section added to our previous ternary example in **Appendix 1.**

EXPANDING YOUR MUSICAL FORM

If we use our own ternary form piece as a starting point (see **Appendix 1**) then we can confidently say that we have fulfilled the criteria on our composition checklist. However, it isn't the most exciting piece of music. There is room to **develop** our ideas into something more stylish. So we'll add another point to our checklist:

- Do the musical ideas develop?

Thankfully, using schemata means that our initial ideas already allow for development of material because they are structured in a way that organically leads from opening ideas, to responding ideas, to contrasting ideas, to closing ideas. Our job now is to expand the piece we already have by using some tried and tested schemata and cadences that we haven't yet explored. In **Part III**, we will look at some ways to elaborate these sketches at a more detailed level. By tackling the overall form first, your sketches will combine and unfold with clarity, purpose, and a sense of direction, coming together in a sophisticated score. The fine detail can be added later.

During the eighteenth century it was very common for pieces of music to be constructed from symmetrical phrases where 2+2=4, 4+4=8, and so on. This kind of regular structure helped give music a sense of balance and clarity. In the more developed music of the Classical period, composers found ways to elaborate these symmetrical patterns. One way they did this was by using a range of delaying techniques – musical tricks that hold off the arrival of strategic cadences, keeping the listener in suspense for a little longer. Here, we are placing these techniques into two broad categories:

1. Standing still

First, we will outline a schema that we have not yet looked at – the Quiescenza. Its job is to make the music seem to pause or stand still by prolonging one harmony. This is useful when you want to stretch out a moment in your piece before moving on – like pausing to reflect before turning to the next chapter in a story.

2. Cadential deferral

Secondly, we will introduce some cadential techniques that cause a rupture or a fault in the approach to a cadence. Composers would sometimes hint at a cadence but then withhold some of the ingredients of closure to stop the music from ending too soon. These include gestures such as evaded and interrupted cadences as well as strategic chord inversions. The result is that the music seems to say, 'Not yet, there's still more to come.'

By using these techniques you will find that your compositions quickly develop from regular, symmetrical statements to elaborate, witty, and dynamic musical narratives.

 # STANDING STILL SCHEMA: THE QUIESCENZA

There are certain points within a piece of music where it is necessary to stand still on the tonic for a moment. This is where the **Quiescenza** (pronounced '**kwee**-uh-**shen**-zah') comes in. This is an especially useful schema when expanding the form of your piece and a beautiful way of generating a sense of stillness or reflection as it rests on ①, giving the tonic some space to unfold. This can be right at the beginning of a piece in order to establish a key, or it might be immediately after a cadence in order to provide a reflective space before moving on to something else. It can also act as a musical epilogue, reinforcing a sense of finality after a perfect cadence.

The main feature of the Quiescenza is the bass pedal on ①, which gives it its sense of stasis and solidity. In the upper voices there are two options:

1. A simple ascending line with **❺**-**❻**-**❼**-**❶** in the melody.

2. A chromatic version with ♭**❼**-**❻**-♮**❼**-**❶** (this is the more common version).

These two options can be used in a simple two-voice texture, or they can be harmonised with chords I, IV, V, and I over the static bass:

Diatonic Quiescenza   **Quiescenza with ♭❼**

The great strength of the Quiescenza is its ability to mark out a key very clearly. For this reason, it is often used as the starting point for a piece of music in a similar way to the other 'opening gesture' schemata we have already looked at, such as the Romanesca, the Do-Re-Mi, and the Meyer.

The Quiescenza in action

The example below shows the opening bars of J.S. Bach's suite for unaccompanied cello. Bach uses figuration in semiquavers to prolong each of the stages of the Quiescenza. The bass is where we expect it to be – the lowest voice in the texture, remaining static on ① – and the **❺**-**❻**-**❼**-**❶** motion can be seen in the 'middle' voice. The 'top' voice fills in the other notes in the harmony (compare with the prototype in the example above).

J.S. Bach: *Cello Suite No. 1 in G Major*

Musical references:
Bach, J. S.: *Cello Suite No. 1 in G Major*, BWV 1007, Prélude, bars 1–4

Another option for an opening statement could be to use the chromatic version, which was much more common in the Classical and Romantic periods. In the example below, Mozart opens his *Piano Sonata in F major* with a Quiescenza. This example is more complex than J.S Bach's. First, Mozart uses the chromatic version with ♭❼. This produces a richer and more complex harmonic profile. Secondly, Mozart uses the Quiescenza as a framework in the accompaniment pattern, but he writes a melody over the top using notes from each of the chords. It might seem unusual to introduce a note outside of the key this early in a piece, but this was very common in galant music.

Mozart: *Piano Sonata in F Major*

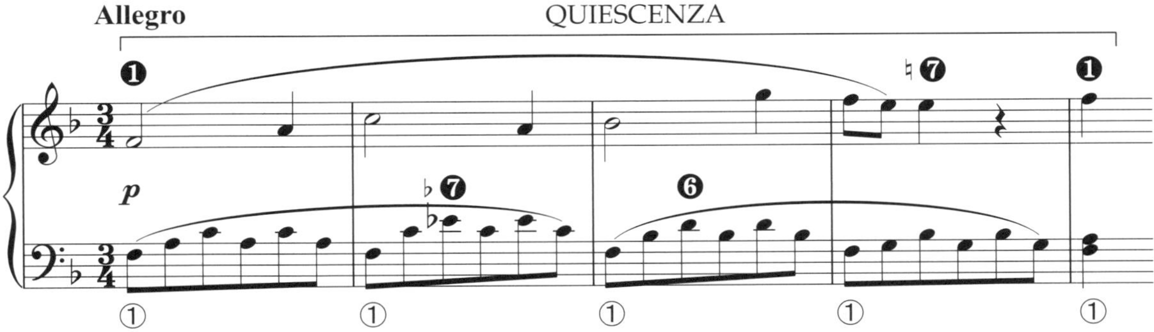

The Quiescenza in other musical styles

The Quiescenza is also found quite commonly in popular music.

I'm Still Standing by Elton John opens with a Quiescenza twice in a row during the song's minor-key introduction, and the first line of the verse, now in the major mode, also uses this schema, minor key intro [0:00–0:11]; major key verse [0:11–0:16].

Elton John is a fan of using schemata in his compositions – after all, he is a classically trained musician! Another clear example, this time from a film, can be heard in *Circle of Life* from *The Lion King* (Elton John/Tim Rice/Hans Zimmer). Here, the diatonic Quiescenza is used at the start of the song, verse [0:49–1:01].

Also highly effective when used in film music, John Williams' *Raiders March* (from *Raiders of the Lost Ark*) features an opening quiescenza [0:00–0:007] that establishes the key with drive and anticipation before the main theme unfolds. The piece is also a good example of a ternary (ABA) structure, with the contrasting B section providing thematic and dynamic contrast.

Special Case: The 'Mannheim Roller'

While the Quiescenza typically creates a sense of stillness, it doesn't always have to. In the eighteenth century, and in response to the symphonic style that was developed at the court in Mannheim by Johann Stamitz and others, it was stylish and exciting to combine the Quiescenza with an upward melodic 'wedge' and a long crescendo. It had the effect of building musical energy. This **Mannheim roller** was quickly adopted by the Viennese school. The example used near the start of Mozart's *Piano Concerto No.16* is as clear and dramatic as any.

Musical references:
Mozart, W. A.: *Piano Sonata No. 12 in F Major*, K. 332, i, bars 1–5
John, Elton/Taupin, Bernie: *I'm Still Standing*: [0:00–0:11], [0:11–0:16]
John, Elton/Rice, Tim/Zimmer, Hans: *Circle of Life* from *The Lion King* [0:49–1:01]

A Mannheim Roller in Mozart: *Piano Concerto No.16*

The Quiescenza is often found at the end of a longer passage, section, or even an entire piece. When it appears immediately after a perfect cadence, it reinforces the sense of finality, giving it the unusual status of something that occurs after the end. It can be thought of as an epilogue, comparable to the moment after a book or film has clearly finished, when the words *THE END* appear.

In music, a perfect cadence usually makes it clear that a passage has ended, but there is often a short idea that follows. This is sometimes called a **codetta** – a brief passage that comes *after the end* of a longer span of music – this role is frequently filled by a Quiescenza. When a Quiescenza appears at both the beginning and the end of a passage, it creates a framing effect, contributing to a sense of Classical balance and symmetry.

> The **codetta** is a statement that occurs after a passage of music has been structurally closed by a perfect cadence. A common feature of codettas from the eighteenth century is the use of a tonic pedal. Once a perfect cadence has been achieved, the bass does not move away from ①, but lingers there for a short time. It was common for composers to build this tonic pedal into a Quiescenza, or more idiomatically, two Quiescenze in a row. We can therefore say that the Quiescenza schema is not a cadence, but that it does the job of prolonging the tonic after a cadence has been reached.

The codetta in other musical styles

Debussy – *Arabesque No.1* (end): Traditional codetta over a tonic pedal, gently rounding off the section and reinforcing tonal stability.

Thomas Newman – *American Beauty* (2:46 onwards): A brief, closing flourish after a formally complete passage, emphasizing the reflective mood with minimal melodic material.

Hamilton – *Who Lives, Who Dies, Who Tells Your Story* (2:58 onwards): Codetta-like affirmation of the tonic (although not a strict tonic pedal), giving closure and reinforcing the key at the end of the phrase.

Musical references:
Mozart, W. A.: *Piano Concerto No.16 in D*, K.451, i, bars 1–10

The Quiescenza after a perfect cadence

Using a Quiescenza after a perfect cadence was so common in the eighteenth century that it almost became a cliché of the galant style. It could be used to calm things down after the excitement of the drive towards closure, or it could equally be used to sustain a high level of musical energy. When used after a cadence, it is normal to hear the Quiescenza twice in a row for extra effect:

Haydn: *Surprise Symphony*

TASK

1. Go back to your composition from **Part II**. Decide if you would like to expand your form **before the start** or **after the end**.

2. Write a bass line that holds a static pedal on ① for at least two bars.

3. In the upper voices, choose one of the two options below. Add the notes to the upper voice, deciding whether you would like the whole pattern to last for four bars (in which case you would have one event per bar) or two bars (two events per bar):

   a. ❺-❻-❼-❶

   b. ♭❼-❻-♮❼-❶

4. Add chords I-IV-V-I underneath each of the melodic events to harmonise the schema.

5. Experiment with repeating the schema to expand the idea even further.

6. If using it at the start of your composition, you may also like to turn it into a Mannheim Roller by adding a crescendo and ensuring the upper voice is ascending by step over the Quiescenza pattern.

Musical references:
Haydn, Joseph: *Symphony No. 94 in G, 'Surprise'*, iii, bars 50–62

CADENTIAL DEFERRAL

Delaying or disrupting the arrival of a cadence is an extremely common tool in music. Cadences are structurally crucial but equally important is the ability to withhold that closure. By delaying the cadence, either momentarily or repeatedly, we are able to extend phrases, spin out ideas, or maintain tension. The delaying tactics that composers used in the eighteenth century fall more or less into three categories: 1) getting stuck on the predominant harmony, 2) the melody does not progress to ❶, steering away from resolution, and 3) the bass does not progress to ①, derailing harmonic closure. Each strategy alters the cadence itself, making it seem as though the music nearly resolved before veering off, asking for more time, or beginning again. We will look at each strategy in turn, sketching out some ideas in our worked example as we go.

Chromatic predominant chords

The most straightforward way to approach the dominant ⑤ in preparation for a cadence is diatonically, meaning using notes and chords that belong to the key. However, eighteenth-century composers sometimes approached ⑤ using chromatic harmony, that is, using notes and chords that sit outside the key for specific effect. The three most common chromatic predominant chords – each with its own expressive flavour – are the **diminished 7th**, the **Neapolitan 6th**, and the **augmented 6th**.

Diminished 7th

Perhaps the most familiar is the diminished 7th chord, a tense, unstable chord made up of a stack of minor thirds. In the galant repertoire, composers typically built the chord up on the bass note ♯④, creating a dramatic chromatic pull towards ⑤.

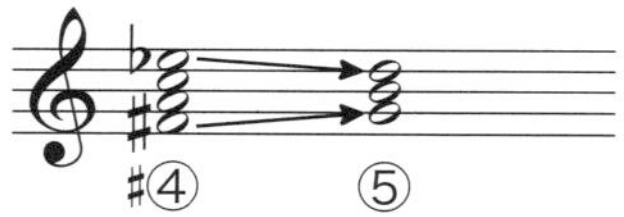

Listen to the Beatles' *Michelle* at 0:15 for an example of a diminished 7th in pop music.

Sometimes composers stopped on the diminished 7th to create a moment of hesitation before pushing forward to the cadence. This gesture emphasises how close the music has come to resolving, only to get temporarily stuck on the static diminished 7th.

Haydn: *Piano Sonata in D Major*

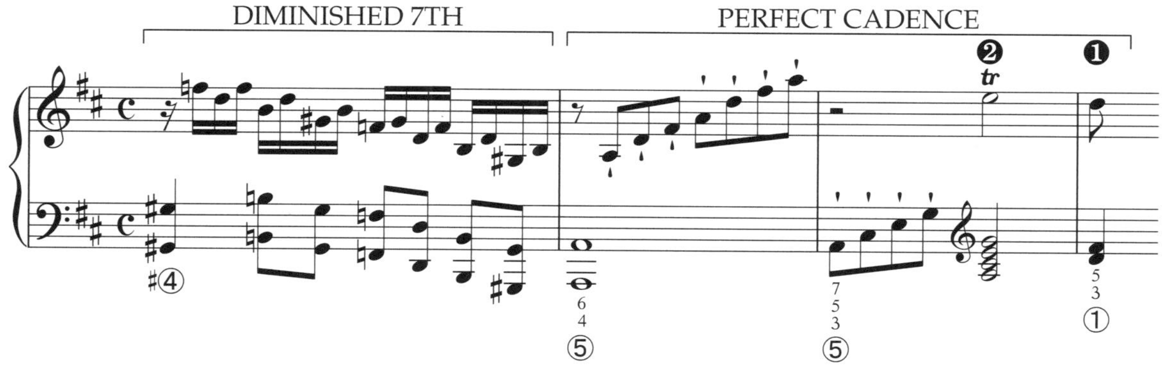

Musical references:
Haydn, Joseph: *Piano Sonata in D Major*, Hob. XVI: 37, i, bars 95-98

Neapolitan 6th

The next chromatic predominant option is the **Neapolitan sixth**. The term *Neapolitan* comes from its frequent use by composers in Naples, and the chord is built on the flattened supertonic (♭2). In a major key, this produces a major triad; for example, in C major the Neapolitan chord is D♭–F–A♭. Although it can appear in root position, it is most commonly used in first inversion (6/3), which is what the "*sixth*" in the name refers to.

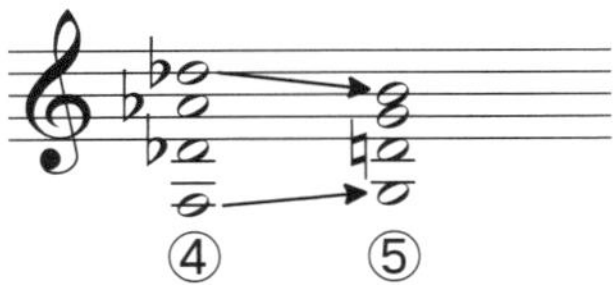

The use of the first inversion means that ④ is the bass note, but the harmony produces a dark, shadowy effect that composers knew how to exploit, especially at tense or dramatic moments. The Neapolitan 6th can be used as a simple alternative to the subdominant in the progress towards a cadence, or as with the diminished 7th, the composer may decide to linger on it for a moment.

A Neapolitan 6th in Schubert: *Quartettsatz in C minor*

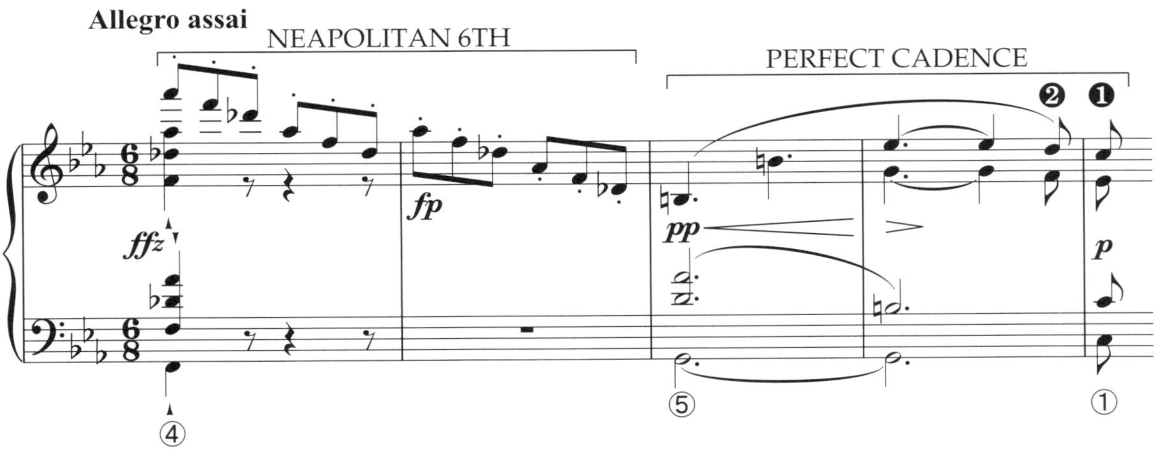

Neapolitan 6th in popular music

There is a good example of a Neapolitan 6th in *Hello* by Lionel Ritchie. In the chorus, the Neapolitan chord is heard under the lyrics "you're all I've ever [wanted]" and "I want to tell you [so much]". This repeats at the same place in subsequent choruses [0:38–1:16].

Linkin Park – *Don't Stay*: Prominent C major (♭II) chords in B minor during the verses. It blurs the line with being in the Phrygian mode, but the effect is Neapolitan-like tension before resolving.

Lady Gaga – *G.U.Y.* [1:09]: Uses a flattened supertonic (♭II) for dramatic effect, giving a Neapolitan flavour in a pop context.

Hans Zimmer – *Dune* soundtrack: In this film music example Phrygian (♭II) chords create a dark, oppressive atmosphere, showing the Neapolitan sonority used for expressive effect rather than Classical structural function.

Musical references:
Schubert, Franz: *Quartettsatz in C minor*, D.703, bars 9–13

Augmented 6th

The next chromatic predominant option is the augmented sixth chord. The term augmented comes from the interval of an augmented sixth between the outer notes of the chord, which resolves outward to the dominant. This chord is built on the flattened sixth (♭⑥) scale degree. For example, an augmented sixth chord resolving to G major might contain A♭, C, and F♯, which move to G, B, and G: the outer notes move outward by semitone while the middle note resolves down to B. The resulting harmony therefore features motion from ♭⑥-⑤ in the bass and ♯④-⑤ in the melody. It is most commonly used in first inversion (6/3), which is what the "*sixth*" in the name refers to.

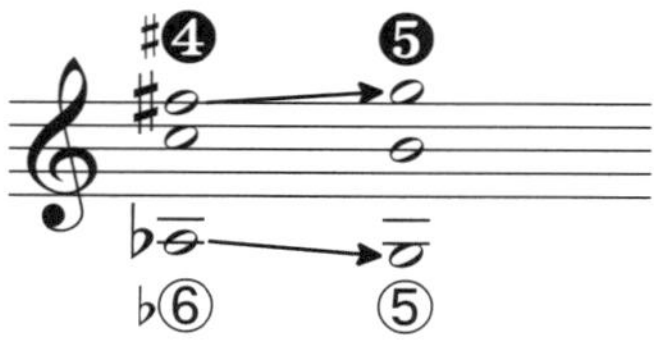

This motion can then progress to ① if desired, or you might choose to wait on the augmented 6th chord for a moment in order to prolong the drama.

An augmented 6th in Mozart: *Overture to Der Schauspieldirektor*

TASK

1. Go back to your composition from **Part II** and locate a perfect or an imperfect cadence.

2. Sketch out some different examples of a chromatic predominant chord to elaborate the cadence. Position your predominant just before ⑤ in your cadence.

   a. Diminished 7th

   b. Neapolitan 6th

   c. Augmented 6th

3. Choose which of these suits the mood and character of your work-in-progress the best and add it in.

Musical references:
Mozart, W. A.: *Overture to Der Schauspieldirektor*, K.486, bars 107–111

EVADED AND INTERRUPTED CADENCES

As a phrase approaches a cadence, we naturally begin to expect a point of arrival. The most straightforward option is to satisfy that expectation by ending the phrase in one of the ways explored in **Part I.** Just as often, however, composers deliberately hold back the ending – disrupting the cadence at the last moment before finally allowing it to resolve.

The evaded cadence

When this surprise happens in the melody, this is called an **evaded cadence**. The melody seems as though it is going to move to the tonic by step but, at the last moment, moves in the opposite direction, usually to ❸ or ❺.

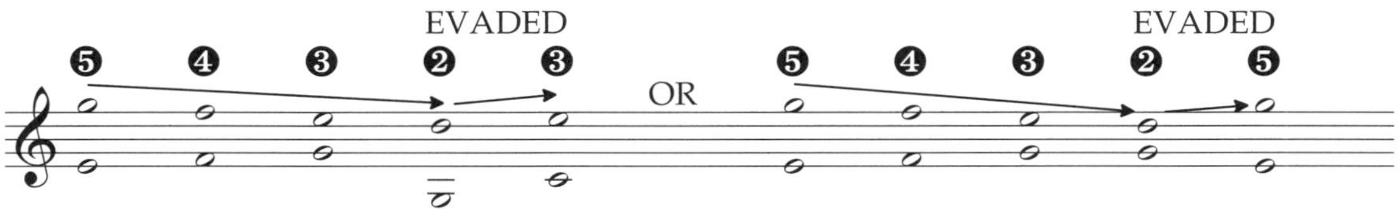

The evaded cadence in action

An evaded cadence in Mozart: *Violin Concerto No.3*

The effect of an evaded cadence in Classical music is usually gentle, merely spinning an idea out for a few more bars.

Musical references:
Mozart, W. A.: *Violin Concerto No.3 in G Major*, K.216 ii, bars 36–37

The interrupted cadence

This technique works in a similar way to the evaded cadence, but the effect of interruption is considerably stronger. This is because the 'wrong turn' happens in the bass voice and therefore affects the harmony, not just the melody. To achieve an **interrupted cadence**, the following steps need to be followed:

- Prepare the end of a phrase as though the music will resolve in a perfect cadence through a motion in the bass to ⑤.

- Instead of progressing to ① (the usual option), move to ⑥.

- Ensure the harmony above ⑥ is a root-position triad. In C major the bass line would move from a G (⑤) up to an A (⑥) with an A minor triad above in the harmony.

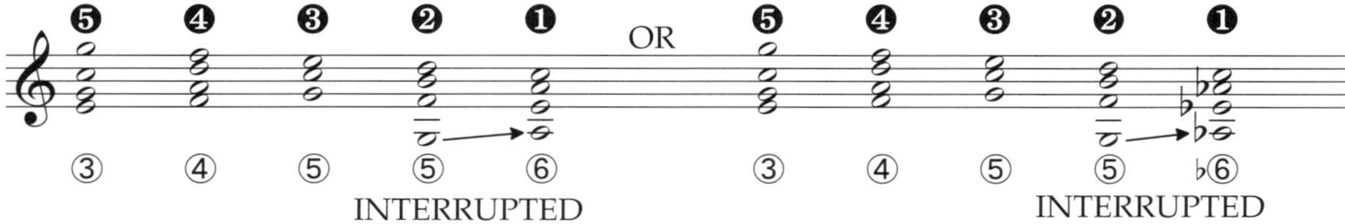

This is especially effective if the bass motion to ⑤ has been stepwise (e.g.③-④-⑤): the music seems to 'overshoot' the dominant and carry on to ⑥, which is heard as literally being a 'step too far'. Sometimes composers used this device several times in a row, with the effect of really wrenching the emotions of the listener.

Interrupted cadences in Mozart: *String Quintet in G Minor*

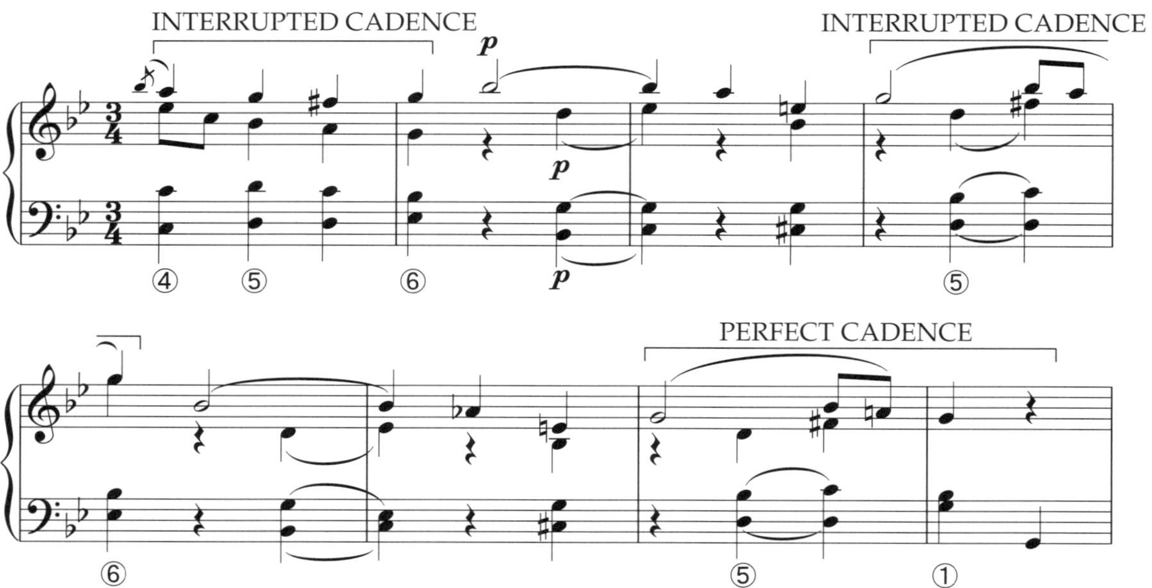

Musical references:
Mozart, W. A.: *String Quintet in G Minor*, K.516, ii, bars 36–43

While evaded and interrupted cadences are very common in galant style and many pieces including Romantic, light music, musical theatre, and pop, they are not considered to be structural in the same way as the imperfect cadence and the perfect cadence. Structural cadences tend to be used quite sparingly, and at the ends of longer passages. A whole sonata movement by Haydn or Mozart might only contain two or maybe three perfect cadences. Developing and evolving your musical ideas is essential for keeping the music engaging and expressive. Let's add this to our checklist:

- Do the musical ideas develop? ✓

By postponing the expected closure, these cadences give the composer space to vary, extend, or transform musical material so it can evolve across the passage and feels like it is growing rather than simply repeating. In this way, evaded and interrupted cadences are not just decorative: they are a tool for demonstrating that ideas can develop within an expanded musical form.

TASK

1. Go back to your composition from **Part II**. Locate a perfect cadence (perhaps at the end of your A section).

2. Sketch out an evaded cadence by using the melody notes ❸-❷-❸ or ❸-❷-❺ above the bass notes ⑤-⑤-①

3. Sketch out an interrupted cadence by replacing the bass note ① of your existing perfect cadence with ⑥, keeping your melody notes the same. You can then repeat it 'one more time', this time ending on ①

4. Choose which of these suits the mood and character of your work-in-progress and add in if it works well.

5. Remember to finish the section of music with a perfect cadence after the interruption or evasion.

USING THE TOOLKIT

To end this chapter, here is a reworking of our original binary form sketch from earlier in **Part II** that incorporates some of the delaying techniques and strategies that we have covered. The piece is now considerably longer as a result of inserting new material at strategic points and by using some delaying techniques. It has grown from a short but structurally coherent 16 bars at the beginning of **Part II** to a much more substantial 42 bars.

Bars	Technique	Notes
7–8	Evaded cadence	Melody fails to reach the new tonic of G (❶), instead rising to B (❸) to delay a firm arrival in G major
8–10	One more time; Perfect cadence	Reattempts G major cadence from bar 9, this time leading to a perfect cadence
15–16	Augmented 6th chord	A♭ (bass) and F♯ (melody) resolve to a G, re-establish G as ⑤ of C major
17–18	Augmented 6th chord	As above but an octave lower to add variety
23–24	Varied tonic Prinner	In bars 5–7 the music moves away from the tonic via a modulating Prinner. Here, the Prinner stays in the tonic. To avoid repetition, it is varied by: • Adding an arpeggio pattern in the melody (see Part III) • Shifting the register up an octave
25–28	Neapolitan 6th passage	We've already reached the tonic of C which is the goal of the piece, so employing the Neapolitan harmony for a few bars adds some drama and delays the end: • Melody follows a D♭ major chord, which is ♭② • The harmony is in the left hand in first inversion (F in the bass)
28	Diminished 7th chord	Chromatic bass following on from the start of the bar (④-♯④-⑤) and stacked minor 3rds over ♯④ create tension.
30–31	Cudworth cadence + double appoggiatura	Adding a Cudworth cadence involving a double appoggiatura
31–32	Evaded cadence	Top melody voice fails to reach the tonic of C (❶), instead rising to E (❸) to delay a firm confirmation of a C major ending
33–34	Interrupted cadence	Could have finished with a perfect cadence in C major, but instead there is a strong deflection from this in the form of an interrupted cadence, with the bass line moving unexpectedly from ⑤ to ⑥. The cadence is then repeated but this time resolving 'correctly'
35–37	Elongated perfect cadence	The length of each chord in the perfect cadence is doubled to a minim to elongate the approach to the cadence, thereby delaying the arrival of ①
37–42	Codetta using Quiescenza schema	A codetta is added to give more of a sense of finality now that the piece is more substantial. Two Quiescenze (second with the melody rhythm varied) are used for this after the perfect cadence, creating a passage 'after the end' of the music.

Elaborated binary form using techniques covered in Part II

You should now feel confident in taking your initial ideas from **Part I** and expanding them into an established musical form. We have explored various ways of doing this and have encountered different schemata and cadences along the way. But how did composers in the eighteenth century make music that, despite following common patterns, still felt individual and original? Next we'll look at how to effectively elaborate our ideas and develop them into something individual and exciting.

PART III: ELABORATION

There are several ways to elaborate the basic versions of each schema, and the choices a composer makes will depend on a lot of different contexts. The purpose of the piece is an important consideration. Something written for an academic setting or for a professional ensemble might use more intricate elaborations compared with music for a more general audience, for example, or something for small children to play in an educational setting. Style and historical context also play a role. For instance, a Classical piano sonata by Mozart typically uses clearer, more goal-directed elaborations than a richly ornamented Baroque prelude by J.S. Bach. The instrumentation matters too. Elaboration often varies with tempo, instrumentation, and metre, so a slow piece for an agile instrument like the violin or the flute might be subject to significantly more elaboration than, for example, a fast piece for double bass or tuba.

In this section we will cover some of the main strategies for elaborating the schemata considering their melody, harmony, and texture. You may want to begin by studying the examples, but don't stop there – the best way to get to grips with the idea of elaboration is to try it for yourself. Improvise at your instrument or sing them out loud, then write your improvisations down as sketches. Elaboration is an active compositional technique – it is not something to work out only in your head or on paper. It grows from direct, physical engagement with sound. As we progress through **Part III**, we will be adding a final point to our 'good composition' checklist:

- **Does the piece demonstrate good control of musical elements?**

ELABORATION OF MELODY

You should now be familiar with the idea that each schema consists primarily of two voices: melody and bass. Either of these can be directly elaborated, though usually it will be the melody that receives the most attention. There are three basic ways of elaborating a melody. In order of complexity, these are: **rhythmic elaboration**, **arpeggiation**, and **scalic elaboration**.

Rhythmic elaboration

We will start with the most basic. Elaborating a shape through **rhythm** simply involves adding a more complex rhythm to the schema's basic profile. This might involve changing note values to be longer or shorter depending on the context. More commonly, each event in the schema stays the same length. Rhythmic patterns are added to give the music more movement.

Rhythmic elaboration in action

In the next example from Mozart's *Haffner Symphony*, you can see that he chooses the Romanesca schema with a leaping bass in A major. In this case Mozart uses a crotchet and two quavers for each stage of the schema, giving the passage energy and character. He elaborates this even further a few bars later, with a quaver pattern which helps to intensify the schema, making it sound more urgent as the music reaches its goal: a perfect cadence in A major.

Mozart: *'Haffner' Symphony*

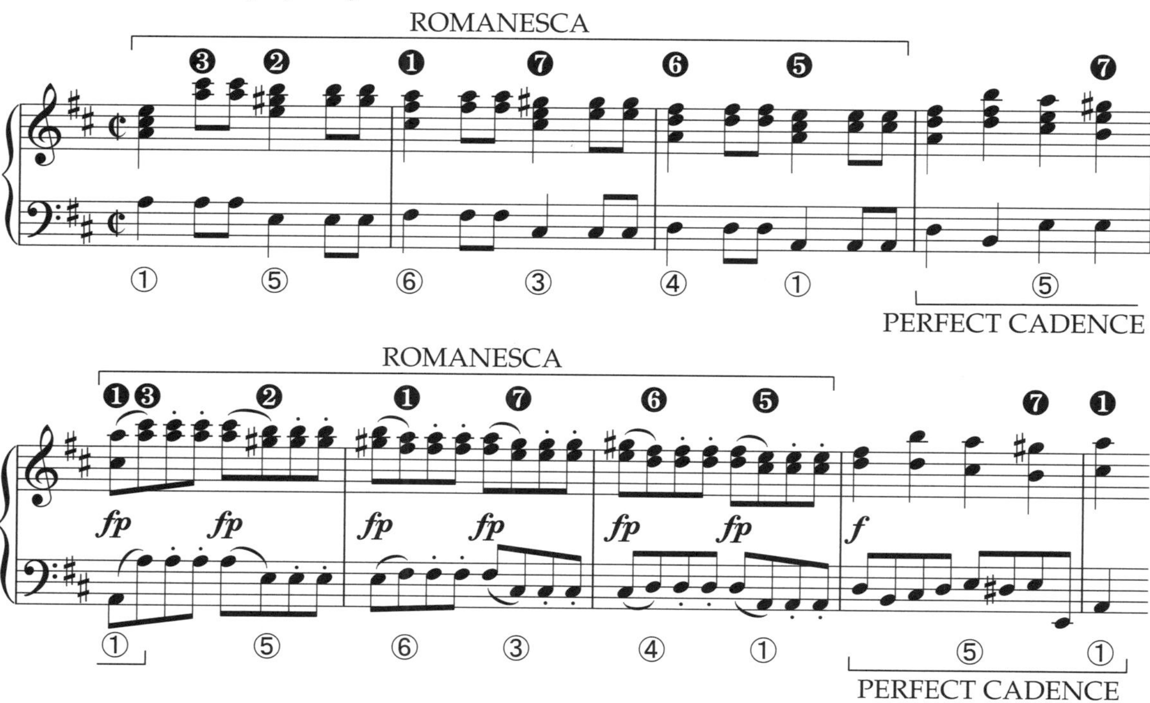

Here is another example of a Romanesca, this time by Corelli, in which the composer has varied the length of each event and elaborated each stage simply by adding a rhythm and rests without changing the core tones of the schema.

Corelli: *Concerto Grosso No.7*

Ultimately, the goal is to avoid repeating ideas in exactly the same way. While we can use a change in schema (or repetition of schema) to guide us to change the rhythm, there are plenty of examples from other genres that demonstrate the same principle – if an idea is repeated, vary it somehow!

Rhythmic elaboration in music for the screen

An example of rhythmic elaboration can be heard in the theme from the TV series *Game of Thrones* by Ramin Djawadi. The first and second time the theme is heard, the rhythm of the second phrase follows the compound time signature, but the third time, when the strings are added to the melody, the end of the phrase is changed to a duple rhythm crossing the beat.

Musical references:
Mozart, W. A.: *Symphony No.35 in D Major, 'Haffner'*, K.385, iv, bars 59–67.
Corelli, Arcangelo: *Concerto Grosso in D Major*, Op.6, No.7, i, bars 1–3.
Djawadi, Ramin: *Main Title from Game of Thrones* [0:00–0:59]

ARPEGGIATION

Another method for elaborating a melody is **arpeggiation**, where a melody note in the schema is developed by leaping to other notes of the same chord, creating melodic interest. In the first movement of his *Piano Sonata in E Major*, Beethoven elaborates the Quiescenza schema by adding a second melody note for each stage of the schema. You'll notice that the first minim of each bar is the core tone of the Quiescenza, in the pattern ❺-❻-❼-❶, while the second note fills out the harmony with arpeggiation. The exception to this is the final ❶ which is only reached right at the end of the pattern, and in a higher register than the rest of the schema. This was normal practice in the eighteenth century and was used by composers to make the schemata more flexible.

Beethoven: *Piano Sonata in E Major*

In the following example by Haydn, the Do-Re-Mi schema is elaborated with an upbeat to precede the ❶. Haydn arpeggiates up to a high D, embellishing the G major harmony. Although one note (F♯) lies outside of the G major triad, it functions as an appoggiatura or lower neighbouring note, resolving neatly to G. You'll see that Haydn uses some more modest arpeggiation in the remainder of the schema, along with more appoggiaturas. The opening flourish, however, is the most memorable part, and it is this that provides the motivic basis for the rest of this passage.

Haydn: *String Quartet in G Major* (piano reduction)

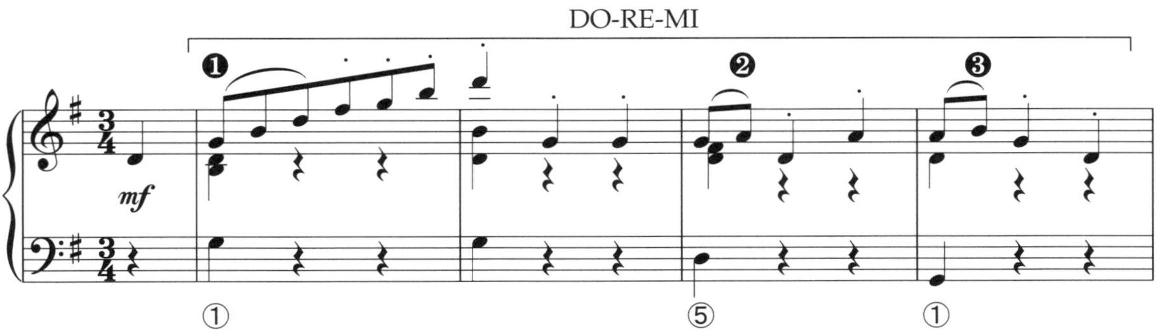

SCALIC ELABORATION

Finally, the most common way of elaborating a basic schematic shape is through **scalic elaboration**. This involves filling the space between the schema's core tones with stepwise motion. This is also the most complex type of melodic elaboration because it introduces dissonance – notes that do not belong to the harmony – and therefore creates a clash. Most of the time we do not notice that there is a clash

Musical references:
Beethoven, Ludwig van: *Piano Sonata in E Major,* Op.14, No.1, i, bars 1–4
Haydn, Joseph: *String Quartet in G Major*, Op.76, No.1, iii, bars 40–44

because composers tend to use smooth, stepwise motion to move between the different points of stability (harmony notes) in a passage.

In this example by Corelli, the notes of the Romanesca melody are connected first by stepwise motion and then by arpeggiation through the notes of the chord. This combination gives the passage shape and character while remaining within the boundaries of the schema.

Corelli: *Concerto Grosso in F Major* (piano reduction)

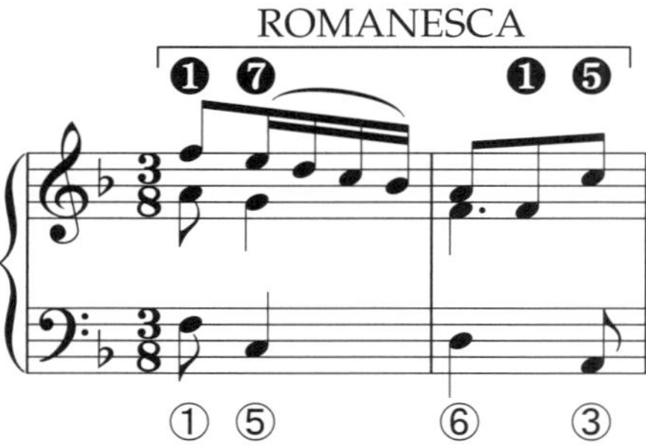

In some more advanced pieces of music, composers would combine these approaches to elaboration alongside some more familiar kinds of ornamentation such as trills, turns, mordents, and appoggiaturas. In this example from his *Violin Concerto No.3*, Mozart varies the elaboration of a Prinner with a mixture of stepwise motion, leaping between notes of the same chord, trills, appoggiaturas, and neighbouring notes. You'll notice in this example that each stage of the Prinner lasts for a whole bar of music. This is because the amount of elaboration that Mozart has decided to introduce requires time to unfold. If this Prinner had been left undecorated (i.e. using only semibreves) it would sound quite plain and uninteresting. By elaborating the melody (note that the bass voice only uses notes of the basic schema), Mozart brings the passage to life.

Mozart: *Violin Concerto No.3* (piano reduction)

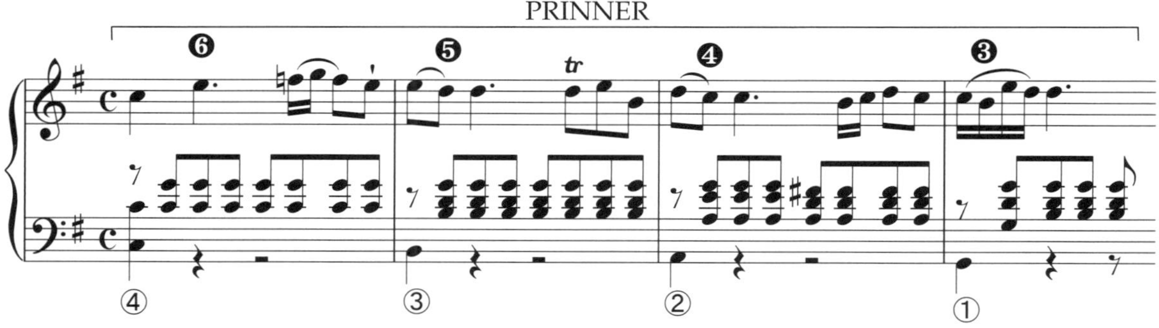

Scalic elaboration and arpeggiation in jazz

As with rhythmic elaboration, there are many examples of scalic elaboration and arpeggiation in music outside of the eighteenth-century context.

The famous jazz standard *Take Five* was composed by Paul Desmond and recorded by the Dave Brubeck Quartet in 1959. The $\frac{5}{4}$ metre distinguishes it from classical examples, but the underlying shape of the Prinner is clearly used to support the central section of the ternary form 'head'. For each of the notes of the Prinner we can hear that Desmond has alternated between using arpeggiation and scalic motion, including some chromatic notes, to decorate and elaborate the melody.

Musical references:
Corelli, Arcangelo: *Corelli: Concerto Gross in F Major*, Op.6, No.9, vi, bars 1–2
Mozart, W. A.: *Violin Concerto No.3 in G Major*, K.216, i, bars 138–141
Desmond, Paul: *Take Five* [0:35–0:49]

We can also revisit the theme tune from the children's television series *Thomas the Tank Engine*. In this case, unlike in *Take Five*, each note of the Prinner's melody is elaborated by arpeggiating upward through the chord rather than downward. This means that each arpeggiation *arrives* at the core tone, rather than starting from it.

TOOLKIT: A WORKING EXAMPLE

Applying rhythmic and melodic elaboration

In our original theme from the end of **Part I** we used rhythmic elaboration as well as arpeggiations and scales to connect the notes of each schema, creating a fluid and varied musical line that demonstrated development of the more basic shapes.

- Rhythm: repeating the notes of the schema will add a rhythmic profile (in bar 1 we simply repeat the note G in the second half of the bar instead of having a crotchet – rhythmic elaboration can sometimes be very straightforward!).

- Arpeggiation: in the second half of bar 2 the C is the main melody note. Instead of remaining on this note, we leap to another consonant note belonging to the chord: G.

- Scales: the first beat of bar 3 is the start of a Prinner. The main note here is the A at the beginning of the bar, but we decided to go up to the C – another note belonging to the same chord of F major. This would have been a leap, but more interest is added by filling the leap in with the B, creating a stepwise ascent.

Elaboration of melody

- Do the musical ideas develop? ✓
- Does the piece demonstrate good control of musical elements? ✓

Musical references:
O'Donnell/Campbell: *Thomas Theme* (1984 version) [0:19–0:29]

Melodic elaboration in writing for voice

If you are writing for voice, whatever the genre is, lyrics will be the stimulus for the melody. Before you start writing your melody, try saying the lyrics out loud so you can hear where the emphasis falls and get a feel for the rhythm and mood. Syllables or words that are emphasised should land on the strong beats of the bar. Always follow their natural rhythm.

There are some specific ways in which you can elaborate the melody to suit the text such as a technique called **word painting**. This is a way of reflecting the meaning of the words in the music. Here are some examples:

- In the chorus of *Wake Me Up* by Wham!, the melody ascends to reflect the meaning of the title very literally. At the end of the chorus, the phrase, "I wanna hit that high" soars up the octave and holds.

- In Purcell's *Music For A While*, the word "eternal" is represented musically by a long melisma: that is, the melodic line has many notes for just one syllable (in this case, e**ter**nal).

TASK

Here are some short lines of lyrics. Using the steps below, have a go at setting the text and using word painting:

- "My head is spinning"
- "I won't be dragged down"
- "Keep on climbing higher"
- "One step closer"
- "Your silence says it all"
- "Now the world stands still"
- "Heartbeats on the dance floor"

Follow these steps to complete the task:

1. Say the lyrics out loud and underline the words/syllables that are emphasised.

2. Ask yourself if there are any words that could be illustrated musically.

   a. You could manipulate the pitch, rhythm, and/or use melisma (singing a single syllable over several successive notes).

   b. You could also repeat words for emphasis.

3. Improvise to find a melody that fits the line **and** demonstrates some word painting.

Musical references:
Michael, George *Wake Me Up*, chorus [0:35–1:10]
Purcell, Henry: *Music For A While*

# ELABORATION OF TEXTURE

Texture in music refers to the number of voices or musical lines that are active and how they relate to each other. More broadly, it encompasses the ways these voices interact, overlap, and combine to shape the overall sound and character of the music. Until now we have mainly been focusing on deeper levels of musical organisation – schema and musical form – but these structures only come to life if they're expressed through a clear and engaging texture. Without this, music can risk sounding dull (if the texture is too uniform) or confusing (if there are too many irrational changes).

All textures combine a 'horizontal' aspect (the melodic line, or combination of melodic lines) and a 'vertical' aspect (the chords that these lines produce). Some textures emphasise one or the other aspect, but as composers we must keep in mind both of these. Just as a beautifully written melody would be no good with haphazard accompaniment, well-considered harmony cannot support a bland and uninspiring melody.

There are some technical categories for the different kinds of musical textures that are useful to guide our choices as composers:

- **Monophony:** a single melodic line, performed by one voice/ instrument, or several in unison.

- **Counterpoint:** the technique of combining two or more independent musical lines (voices/ instruments) so that they harmonise and interact rhythmically. (When used as an adjective: contrapuntal.)

- **Polyphony:** meaning 'many sounds' in which multiple independent lines are heard simultaneously. Polyphony is similar to counterpoint, but the term is usually applied descriptively, especially to early music (before c.1600).

- **Homophony:** several voices moving together to make a series of chords. Church hymns and Christmas carols tend to be homophonic.

- **Melody and accompaniment:** a single melodic voice emphasising the horizontal component of musical texture, with a bass and harmonic filling emphasising the vertical (chordal) component.

There are also some stock textures that are found commonly in the repertoire that can be borrowed and used freely when writing in different styles. The two key questions for this section, then, are:

1. What kinds of texture should I use for my piece?

2. How do I know when to change the texture?

We are composing using galant schemata, and so the starting point is a very basic form of two-part counterpoint with the melody tones above (e.g. ❶-❷-❸) and the bass tones below (e.g. ⑥-⑤-①). Here are some increasingly extravagant examples of a Prinner using different keyboard textures, purely to demonstrate the endless possibilities that can result from a simple two-part texture:

Prinner with different examples of surface texture

1. Homophonic chordal texture

2. Contrapuntal texture with suspensions

3. Melody and accompaniment texture with broken-chord accompaniment

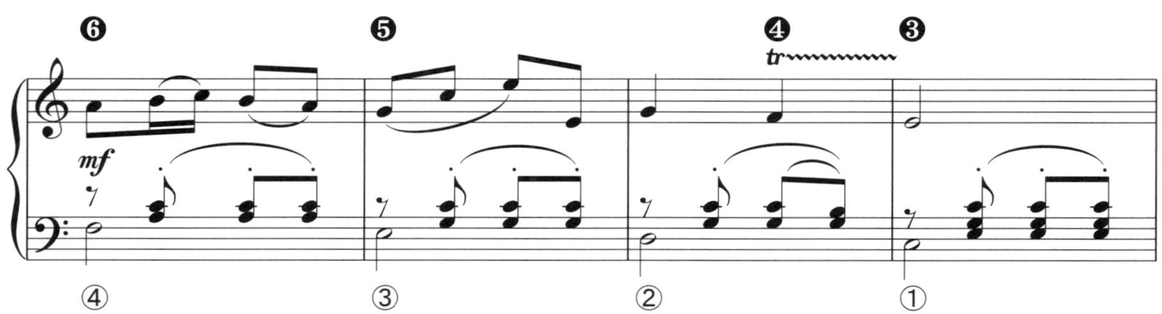

4. Contrapuntal texture with ascending ornamental flourishes.

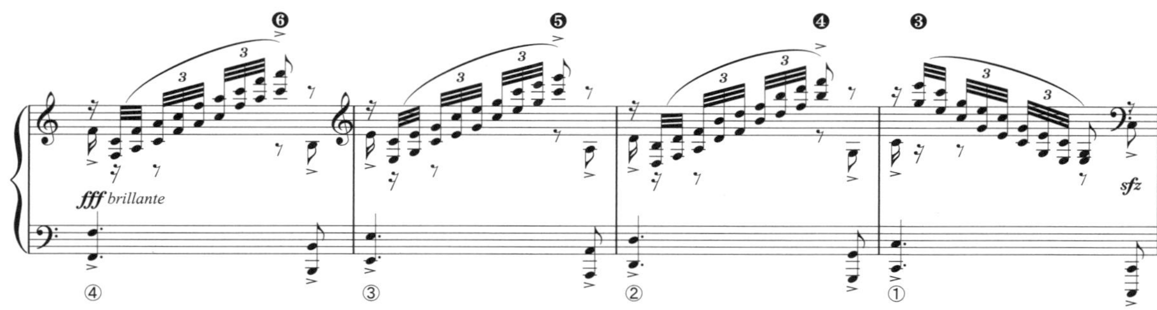

While there are too many potential combinations of instruments for us to cover, the following examples (solo piano, piano plus melody instrument, a duet of two melodic instruments, and small ensemble) demonstrate some of the most important principles of handling instrumental textures.

WRITING FOR KEYBOARD

There is one texture in particular that is closely associated with Classical keyboard music: the *Alberti bass*. Named after the Italian composer Domenico Alberti (c.1710–1746), it involves breaking up a chord into a repeated pattern (often low-high-middle-high, so in C major C-G-E-G), usually in the left hand. Despite its name, the Alberti bass is not a single, linear bass line, but a repetitive, arpeggiated accompaniment pattern. The keyboard instruments of the eighteenth century did not have such a strong sustaining quality as the modern piano, and so it became common to alternate the notes of the chord in the left hand in order to give more of a sense of continuity. Strings, woodwind, and brass are all capable of sustaining a note for a longer time and therefore do not need to mimic the effect for continuity of sound.

Alberti-style figuration is typically used as part of a melody and accompaniment texture. A quick look at the keyboard repertoire from the Classical period shows that most composers did not use it for prolonged periods. In Mozart's *Sonata in C* he uses the texture for the first four bars before moving on to a new texture. You'll notice that the change of texture coincides with the end of one schema and the beginning of another.

Mozart: *Piano Sonata in C Major*

Musical references:

Mozart, W. A.: *Piano Sonata in C Major*, K.545, i, bars 1–12

In the keyboard music of this era composers frequently used a patchwork of different types of musical texture, often changing texture when the underlying schema changes. Let's look at a longer example by Haydn.

Haydn: *Minuet No.11*

Musical references:
Haydn, Joseph: *Minuet No.11*, Hob. ix: 8

This very simple binary form minuet is composed from only three schemata, namely the Sol-Fa-Mi, the Indugio, and the Quiescenza:

Bars	Schema	Key
1–4	Sol-Fa-Mi (❺-❹-❸)	I
5–6	Indugio	I
7–8	Perfect cadence	I
9–12	Quiescenza	V
13–16	Sol-Fa-Mi	I
17–18	Indugio	I
19–20	Perfect cadence	I

To find out more about how to construct a **Sol-Fa-Mi** and **Indugio** schema, see **Appendix 2**

The Alberti-style figuration (albeit playing the low and middle note of the chord simultaneously) is associated only with the Sol-Fa-Mi in bars 1–3. The rest of this short piece consists of a 3-part texture (which expands to four voices only for the cadences) which could be described as a melody and accompaniment. Notice how Haydn does not fill in every single note of the harmony at every stage – he keeps the texture light.

Chord spacing

You'll notice that, in general, smaller intervals like 3rds work well between the voices in the upper register, while wider intervals like octaves and 6ths are used in the lower register. Tightly packed chords in the low register can sound muddy, even if they're easy to play. A good rule of thumb is that the largest gaps should go at the bottom, and the root of the chord is usually the one to double higher up if necessary. Avoid doubling the third of the chord as it makes the music sound too rich.

Alberti bass in video game music

There is a clear example of Alberti bass in the *Ending Theme* from *Super Mario Bros. 2*. It accompanies a simple scalic melody.

TWO-PART KEYBOARD TEXTURE

There is a lot of keyboard music by D. Scarlatti and Cimarosa that keeps to two voices in the main. While Haydn and Mozart used some chords, their music shows that it is not always necessary to spell out the harmony at every stage: the schemata on their own are enough to imply what is going on harmonically.

Two-part texture in action

In the example below, Cimarosa briefly adds an inner voice to flesh out the harmony at the end of bar 6 into bar 7 and again at the end of bar 7 into bar 8. The music is articulating an imperfect cadence at these points, so an extra voice adds some clarity to the harmony. For the main part, Cimarosa sticks to two voices. This is also useful because the music is adaptable for different combinations of instruments.

Musical references:
Kondo, Koji: *Super Mario Bros 2 (Ending Theme)* [starts at 0:34]

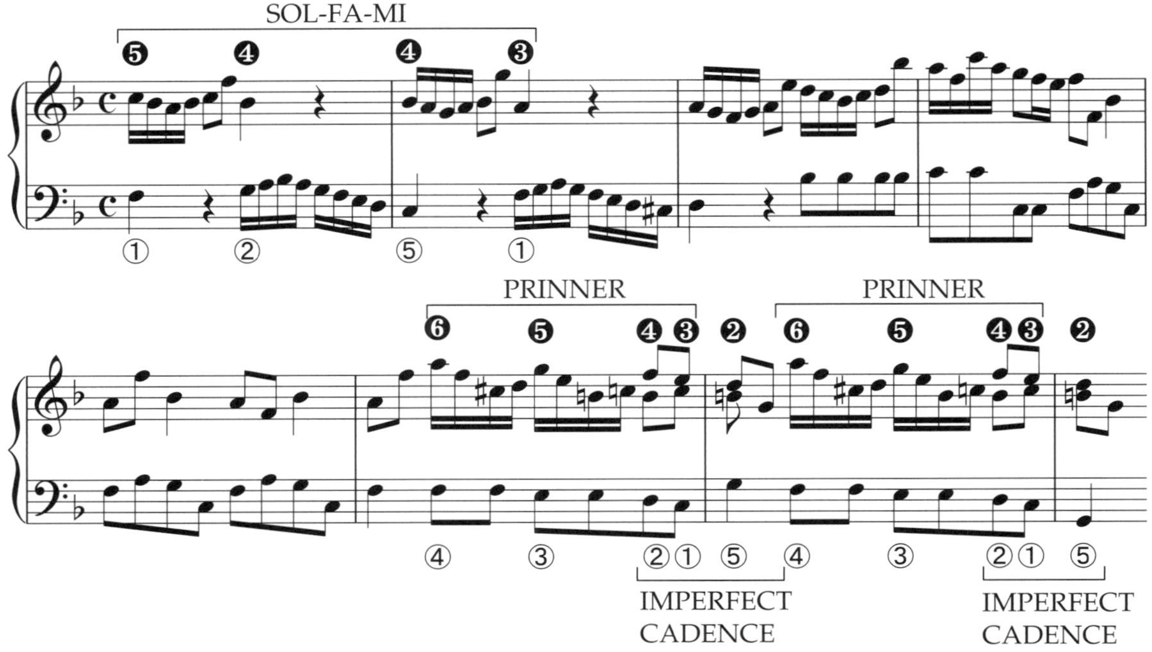

TOOLKIT: A WORKING EXAMPLE

How to write for solo keyboard

- By following the steps in **Parts I** and **II** you will already have a 2-part keyboard texture.

- Keep the emphasis on the melody and bass as they move forward through each schema. If you do need to flesh out the harmony, avoid block chords, especially in a low register. Instead, try arpeggiating through the chord or playing the bass note in the lower register before jumping the left hand up to play chords in the middle register.

- As you approach a cadence, you can intensify the texture by changing from alternating motion to repeated motion by using block chords.

In this example we have taken the start of our piece – a Romanesca and Prinner – and changed the left-hand part to make it more idiomatic for the piano. By arpeggiating the chords rather than writing out blocks of harmony, the texture becomes more delicate and less clunky. Always make sure that the two voices do not bump into each other!

Elaboration of texture (keyboard)

Musical references:
Cimarosa, Domenico: *Keyboard Sonata in F Major*, C.24 bars 1–8

Alternative elaboration of Romanesca-Prinner (keyboard)

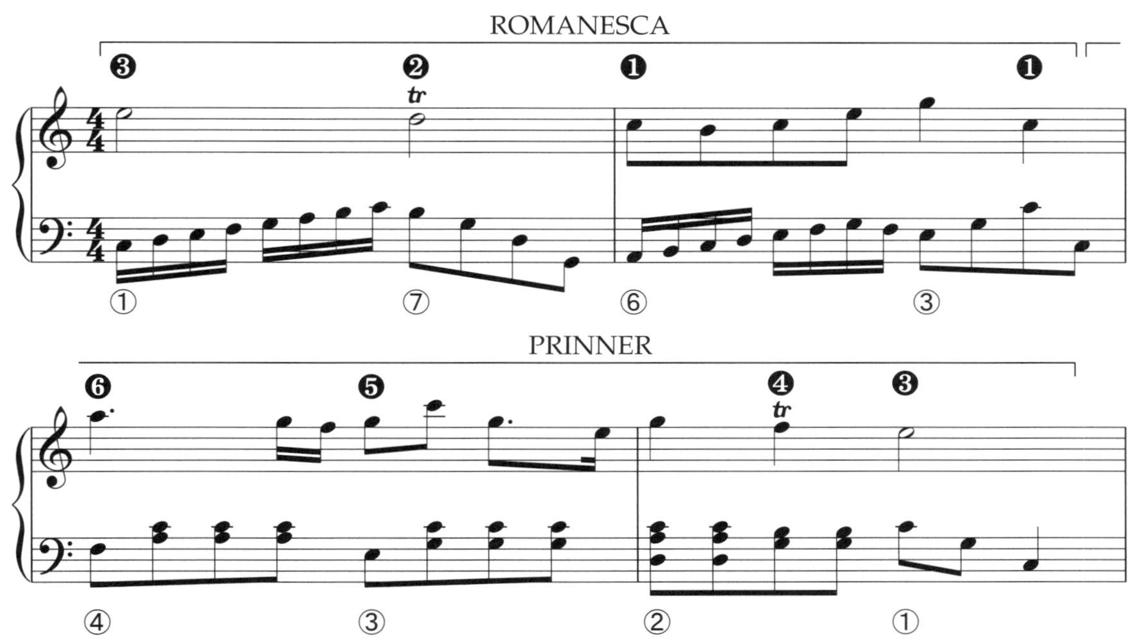

In this alternative example using new material for a Romanesca-Prinner pathway, we have chosen to elaborate the bass line more than the melody to begin with. We have changed the texture with the change of schema, and have avoided muddy triads in the left hand by splitting the harmony into a bass note and accompaniment pattern. In the final bar, in order to emphasise the approach to the cadence, we have switched to repeated chords which give the accompaniment more sense of direction.

TASK

Turn to your composition. Revisit where the different schemata happen and alternate between an Alberti bass figuration, two-part texture, and simple chords. Play around with this to find a combination of textures that works for you.

Piano textures in Romantic and 20th-century music

We've looked at examples of galant-style 2-part texture but here are some examples of different piano textures you might like to explore.

Schumann – *Von fremden Ländern und Menschen*: A lovely example of voice leading and texture, with intricate inner lines that float beneath the melody, showing how expressive two- and three-part writing can be.

Chaminade – *Romance, Op. 40 No. 1*: Features a prominent left-hand melody demonstrating how texture can be used to create intimacy and lyricism.

Satie – *Gymnopedie No. 1*: Avoids the four-chord loops often found in minimalist music, instead relying on subtle harmonic shifts and spacing to create texture and atmosphere.

❖ WRITING FOR PIANO PLUS ONE

Our next example of texture is piano plus another instrument. This could be a combination of piano with a high instrument like a violin or flute, or a low-register instrument like the cello or bassoon.

In the galant style these pieces were considered to be duos and the two instruments acted as equal partners in the texture. Let's take the example of music for piano and violin. It is possible for the violin to play the melody while the left hand of the piano part plays the bass line and the right hand fills in the harmony. It would be equally possible for the violin and the piano right hand to switch roles, so the violin is acting as the accompaniment to the piano melody. In other words, players have the opportunity to play the melody and to do some accompaniment, and this can also have implications for your music's schematic pathway. When the same musical idea returns in a contrasting instrumental colour, the repetition feels fresh because of the change in timbre.

Piano plus one texture in action

Mozart: *Piano Sonata in B♭ Major*

Musical references:
Mozart, W. A.: *Piano Sonata in B♭ Major*, K.378, i, bars 1–16

In this example from Mozart the texture could just as easily have worked as a string quartet. The violinist is playing harmonic figuration that looks like a 2nd violin line in a quartet texture. The piano left-hand part plays something that looks like a viola part, but it also catches a bass note in each bar, with the sustaining pedal helping to prolong that note. The melody is found in the right-hand stave. So, there are clearly four components in this texture – a melody, two harmony parts, and a bass – like a string quartet would have, and with the violin in an accompanying role.

Then, in bar 9 the roles are reversed: the violin plays the melody, the harmony is all in the piano right hand and the left hand plays the bass. You'll notice, though, that the change of texture is strategic: it coincides with a perfect cadence and a repetition of the music from bar 1, allowing both instruments to present the melody and avoiding any risk of the repetition becoming dull.

Romantic and 20th-century sonatas

Here are some sonatas from the Romantic and 20th-century periods that showcase a similar partnership between instruments, with melody and accompaniment roles shared or exchanged.

Brahms – *Clarinet Sonata No. 1*, 1st movement: A Romantic sonata that shares the melodic material between clarinet and piano, showing a true dialogue rather than a soloist/accompaniment model.

Shostakovich – *Cello Sonata*, 2nd movement: Features lively back-and-forth between cello and piano, with the cello alternating between percussive accompaniment and taking over the melody.

Vignery – *Sonata for Horn and Piano*, 1st movement: Shows a true partnership between horn and piano with melodic dialogue, colourful interplay and balanced role reversal.

How to write for piano plus one

1. Think of your texture as being made up of three components: melody, bass, and harmonic filling.

2. If using piano plus a high instrument (violin, flute, oboe, clarinet, trumpet, etc.) then start off by giving the melody to that instrument. This frees up the right hand of the keyboard part to focus on filling in the harmony. Come up with some different ways of varying this: repeating the chords, arpeggiating the chords, and so on.

3. Sometimes it is possible for the melodic instrument to drop into an accompanying role, allowing the right hand of the piano to play the melody. Other ways of varying this texture include:

    a. Give the plus one instrument a rest.

    b Split the melody line between the two instruments, creating a sort of call-and-response texture.

    c. Have one instrument repeat a melodic idea in a different register, e.g. up the octave.

4. If you are writing for piano plus a low instrument (cello, bassoon, tuba, etc.) then the melody should still be given to that instrument initially. Don't get it to play the bass line, which should normally go to the left hand of the piano. Make sure that the melody and the bass do not cross over. Low notes on a deeper solo instrument work best with the piano higher up, creating space for the line to project clearly.

Elaboration of texture (keyboard plus one)

In this example we added a flute to the keyboard texture, raising the melody by an octave. This not only suits the flute's register but also keeps the parts clear and balanced, preventing the texture from becoming too busy or muddy. The left-hand bass remains simple, allowing the other parts to provide enough activity and ensuring the texture stays balanced.

TASK

Turn to your composition and choose a solo instrument to go with the piano. Follow the steps above to arrange your piece for piano with an additional instrument. Experiment with different kinds of accompaniment texture and change the texture strategically when the schemas change.

 # WRITING FOR DUET

When considering which instruments to choose for your duet, it is important to consider things like register, balance, and timbre.

Register

Two instruments with similar registers work nicely, not least because they can cross over from time to time and reverse the roles of melody and bass. The trick here is to make sure that the two lines do not bump into each other. It might be useful when you are sketching out your composition to write both parts on a single stave so that it is clear how the two lines relate to each other. You can then separate them when you come to present your work at the end.

One high instrument and one low is a standard combination. There is less risk of the instruments crossing over now; one bass instrument and one treble is usually a safe choice. Be careful with combinations of instruments that are too distant from one another in register – a duet for piccolo and double bass could give the impression that the lines are coming unstuck from each other and produce some unintended comedic effects.

Timbre and balance

There are two fundamental types of instrumental combination. One approach is to combine two instruments from the same instrumental family. This was a common choice for composers in the eighteenth and nineteenth centuries. Examples include two string instruments (e.g. violin and cello), two wind instruments (e.g. flute and clarinet), or two brass instruments (e.g. trumpet and trombone). Such pairings tend to blend and balance well, producing a unified sonority.

An alternative approach is to combine instruments from different orchestral families. These combinations offer greater contrast in colour and character, allowing composers to explore a wider palette of timbres. While the instruments may blend less closely, this clarity of difference can be used creatively and expressively. Cross-family pairings became increasingly common in the 20th century and are now a defining feature of much contemporary composition. In all cases, the main challenge is achieving a balance of volume and timbre between the two players. Some combinations are therefore less practical in certain contexts: for example, a viola paired with a tuba can be difficult to balance, as the viola may be easily overwhelmed by the tuba's greater power.

Instrumental pairings in Romantic and 20th-century duets

The following duets show how composers can use a variety of pairings – same-family or cross-family – to create dialogue, contrast, and expressive interplay between two instruments.

Rossini – 5 Duets for 2 Horns: *II. Menuetto*: Clear Classical dialogue with melodic and contrapuntal interest.

Delibes – *Flower Duet* (from *Lakmé*): Famous operatic duet; beautifully balanced cross-range pairing.

Clarke – *Prelude, Allegro & Pastorale* for Clarinet and Viola: Cross-family pairing with expressive interplay and timbral contrast.

Bartók – *44 Duets for 2 Violins*: Excellent examples of folk-influenced contrapuntal dialogue.

Poulenc – *Sonata for 2 Clarinets*: Showcases rhythmically playful counterpoint.

Ginastera – *Duo for Flute & Clarinet*: Mid-20th-century work with lively dialogue and timbral variety.

Duet texture in action

In this example by Beethoven, the pairing of clarinet and bassoon achieves a good balance of volume and timbre. There is enough of a difference in register to allow the melody to be clearly heard on the clarinet, while the bassoon plays the bass line. The bassoon part mainly follows an arpeggiated line outlining the notes of each chord.

Beethoven: *Duo No. 1 for Clarinet in C and Bassoon*

Musical references:
Beethoven, Ludwig van: *Duo No. 1 for Clarinet in C and Bassoon*, WoO 27, iii, bars 1–20

How to write for duet

- Stick to the main notes of the schema patterns (melody and bass), with some elaborations.

- Make sure you know the playable range of the two instruments – don't exceed it as the players won't be able to perform your piece!

- Make sure that the voices do not cross over in the middle of a schema. If you are using two instruments that are close in register then they can swap roles of melody and bass between schemas, if you want them to.

Elaboration of Texture (duet)

We chose a mixed combination of instruments for our duet: oboe and cello. As you can see, it is possible to keep the texture very straightforward – plenty of long notes are good because, unlike the piano, cello and oboe are able to sustain the sound well.

TASK

Turn to your composition. Decide whether you would like to write for two instruments from the same orchestral family (strings, wind, or brass), or a mixed duet. Follow the steps above to experiment with this texture.

WRITING FOR SMALL ENSEMBLE

While keyboard music was one of the most common types of composition for galant composers, pieces for small ensembles – chamber music – were also very important. There are many different combinations available for schematic compositions, but in general a group of two, three, or four instruments with a spread of different ranges tends to work well. One bass instrument and two high instruments was common (2 violins + cello, for example), or two high instruments, one middle-register instrument, and one bass instrument also works very well; the structure of a string quartet.

Similar to keyboard writing, composers would normally change the texture at the end of a section, or when moving from one schema to another. It is not idiomatic to change the texture when the music is only part-way through a schema.

String quartet texture in action

Mozart: *String Quartet in D Major*

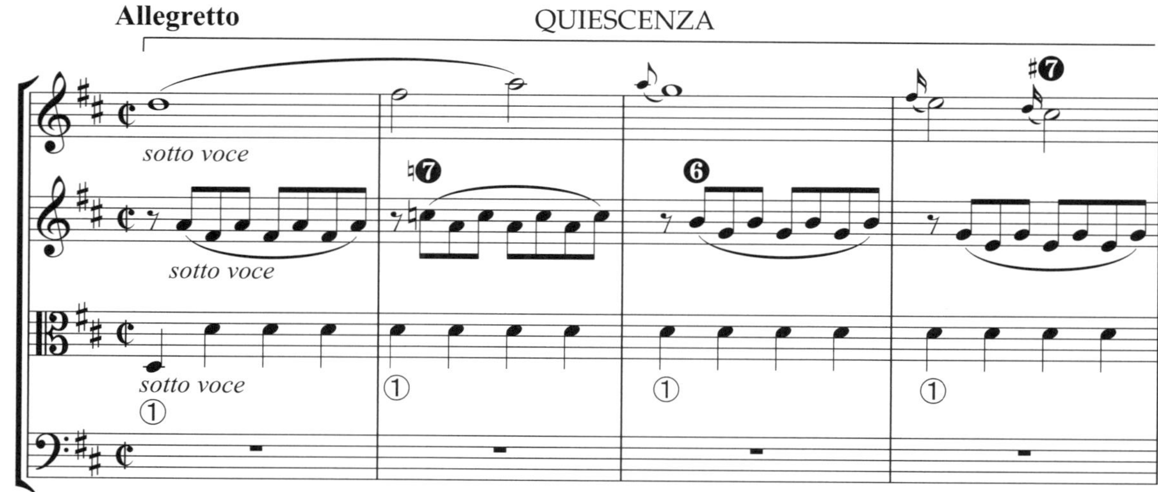

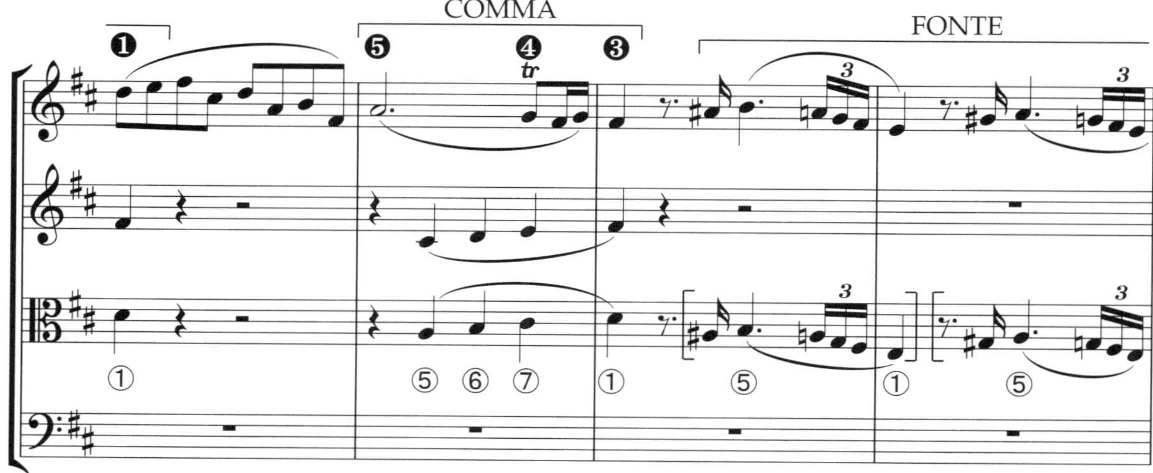

Musical references:
Mozart, W. A.: *String Quartet in D Major*, K.575, i, bars 1–23

COMMA
FONTE
DO-RE-MI
EVADED CADENCE
DO-RE-MI

This example of a string quartet by Mozart shows the strategy quite clearly. The schematic layout with elaborations of the texture is as follows:

Bars	Schema	Texture
1–5	Quiescenza	<ul><li>Three-part texture of melody and accompaniment:<ul><li>Violin I provides melody</li><li>Violin II provides harmony by alternating between notes of the chord</li><li>Viola plays pedal bass line</li></ul></li><li>This texture emphasises the vertical, harmonic aspect of the music</li></ul>
6–7	Comma cadence	<ul><li>Stepwise motion in each voice emphasises the horizontal aspect – the melodic line of the music</li></ul>
7–9	Fonte	<ul><li>Just two instruments playing in octaves</li></ul>
9–13	Quiescenza	<ul><li>Repetition of the Quiescenza from the opening, but this time:<ul><li>Viola provides melody (chamber music is supposed to be fun to play, so it's common for the melody to be passed around the different instruments)</li><li>Violin I *and* Violin II provide harmony</li><li>Cello plays pedal bass line</li></ul></li></ul>
14–15	Comma cadence	<ul><li>Repetition of bars 6–7, but with the melody in the viola</li></ul>
15–17	Fonte	<ul><li>Repetition of bars 7–9, but now an octave higher and played by the two violins</li></ul>
17–19	Do-Re-Mi	<ul><li>Homophonic texture<ul><li>All parts move together (with some minor decoration in the top part)</li></ul></li></ul>
19–21	Evaded cadence	<ul><li>Melody and accompaniment, with long notes in the lower voices</li></ul>
21–23	Do-Re-Mi	<ul><li>Homophonic texture<ul><li>All parts move together (with some minor decoration in the top part)</li></ul></li></ul>

To find out more about how to construct a **Comma cadence**, see **Appendix 2**

You'll notice that each time the schema changes, it is accompanied by a change of texture. You'll also notice that Mozart thought it was perfectly fine for some of the instruments to remain silent at certain points in the music. The pleasing effect of this strategy is that it creates a musical surface that is continuously being varied according to the schematic pattern. By following this logic, your composition will have the effect of constantly refreshing the ear of your listeners.

How to write for string quartet:

- The 1st violin should normally play the melody (although passing it to other parts periodically, as looked at previously, helps to keep the texture fresh).
- The cello should normally play the bass line.
- Use the 2nd violin and viola to add harmony notes in the middle of the texture.
- Think carefully about spacing. Good spacings include:
    a. Four instruments close together (for intensity)
    b. Four instruments widely and evenly spaced (for a spacious effect)
    c. High 1st violin, supported by three lower voices (for a soloistic effect)
    d. Low cello and three high voices
- Avoid two low voices and two high as this creates a gap in the middle.

Elaboration of texture (string quartet)

In our version for string quartet we gave the melody to the 1st violin and the bass to the cello. Unlike the piano versions, which arpeggiate through the chord in the accompaniment, stringed instruments work better by repeating or sustaining the notes of the chord. We set up a semiquaver pattern in the accompaniment that continues to the end of the phrase, after which it might be effective to change it. We also shortened the notes in the cello part, adding in some rests. This adds some air into the texture and prevents it from becoming overscored and muddy.

Alternative elaboration of Romanesca-Prinner (string quartet)

In this alternative example using our new material for a Romanesca-Prinner pathway, we have given the 1st violin the melody while keeping the simple schematic bass outline in the cello part. The 2nd violin and viola parts are then responsible for harmony, so we have opted for an oscillating quaver pattern outlining the notes of the chord, making sure there is no overlap between the parts. We have changed the texture with the change of schema, increasing the momentum in the cello crotchets and adding energy in the inner parts with *staccato* quavers, helping to create a sense of goal-oriented motion towards the end of the phrase.

TASK

We have used lots of examples of quartets in earlier parts of the book but have avoided presenting them in full score (i.e. one part per line) to keep the schemata clear. Go back to some of these examples and find the full score (imslp.org is the place to look). What choices has the composer made in terms of the texture? Do the changes in texture coincide with strategic moments, e.g. changes in schema or arrival of a cadence?

Turn to your composition. Create a string quartet texture for your first 8 bars. Follow the steps in our working example to experiment with this texture, making sure that nothing goes below the bass.

General advice for building textures

- The overriding principle for constructing textures in a Classical style is that the melody and the bass line do not cross. If you are writing for two melody instruments or a simple two-voice keyboard texture, the lines should never cross by accident.

- For bigger textures, think of them in three components: melody, bass, and harmonic filling. Create enough space between the melody and bass for the harmonic filling to go in – this might mean putting your melody up by an octave, or the bass down by an octave.

- Harmonic filling is usually done by the right hand of the piano in piano plus one textures, or by the inner parts of a small ensemble such as 2nd violin and viola in a string quartet. Do not allow the harmonic filling to go below the bass line – this will change the chord inversion and make a nonsense of your schemas.

- Keep the texture clear and uncluttered.

When to vary the texture within the ensemble

Returning now to our first question – how to know which texture to choose at any particular moment – we should return to Mozart's *Piano Sonata in C Major*. The first strategic goal of this sonata is the imperfect cadence that is achieved with the help of a Ponte in bars 11–12 (for more on the **Ponte** schema, see **Appendix 2**). Although Mozart does not indicate how loudly this music should be played, a *crescendo* is implied through the textures that he chooses.

Mozart: *Piano Sonata in C Major*

Musical references:
Mozart, W. A.: *Piano Sonata in C Major*, K.545, i, bars 1–12

Bars	Schema	Texture
1–2	Opening idea	• Alberti-style accompaniment
3–4	Prinner	• This texture emphasises the **vertical**, chordal part of the music
5–8	Prinner	• Still melody and accompaniment, but the intensified flurry of semiquavers in the right hand moves the music forward • This texture emphasises the **horizontal**, or melodic line of the music
9–10	Indugio	• Further intensified through lack of rests in the left hand • Right hand continues driving ahead into bar 10 with continued semiquaver motion
11–12	Ponte	• Even further intensified as semiquavers swap to left hand • Three hammer strokes in bar 12 confirm imperfect cadence (arrival on a chord of G major in the key of C)

Mozart shifts the texture at each transition between schemata, using these changes to escalate the music toward the cadential goal. After bar 12, the intensity drops briefly before building again. Much Classical music follows a similar pattern: starting with a calm texture, intensifying toward each cadential goal, and reserving the greatest weight for the final cadence. To maintain coherence, it's best to change the texture only at schema boundaries or other strategic points.

Approaching texture in other styles

While we have referenced other genres of music, our examples have largely focused on the Western classical tradition. If you are more at home with styles such as jazz, musical theatre or pop, you can take the core principles from this part of the book and transfer them to your preferred style:

- Don't rely too heavily on one texture.
- Use a combination of dense and light textures.
- Aim to change the texture at the points where you change schema.
- Texture can build momentum. Following a build-peak-drop pattern appears everywhere from Mozart sonatas and Beethoven symphonies to film scores and electronic dance tracks.

You can take some stock textural ideas from specific genres:

- **Pop and rock**: use changes in texture to define verse, chorus, and bridge sections.
- **Jazz**: alternate between sparse accompaniment and fuller chordal textures. Think about when everyone will play and when some players will need to take a rest.
- **Film and game music**: play with the intensity by layering instruments to achieve a heavier texture. Think about ways of varying the texture to reflect what is going on in the narrative of the game or the film.
- **Musical theatre**: use changes in texture to distinguish between characters and to respond to the narrative as it develops.

Here is a simple Romanesca-Prinner schematic pathway expanded into a jazz quartet:

To expand our Romanesca Prinner pathway into a jazz ensemble, we first treated it like a keyboard-plus-one texture: the trumpet carried the melody, the piano's left hand the bass line, and the right hand provided harmony with jazz features such as syncopation and added 6ths and 7ths. We reinforced the bass line in the double bass, playing crotchets throughout to create a walking bass an octave below the piano left hand, avoiding interference. Finally, a drum kit layer was added, using a simple pattern on hi-hat, snare, and kick.

These four bars outline the texture typically found in the head of a jazz standard. Contrast in later sections is created by varying how many instruments play at a time. For example, solo sections often feature a single melodic instrument with a pared-back accompaniment, sometimes just on beats 1 and 4.

As we developed the trumpet part, we left out the ❷ that would normally appear in the schema. This occurred naturally while improvising a melody that sounded right for jazz. Not all improvisations or compositions will fit the schema perfectly – that is expected. If the music serves the composition's purpose, whether for an exam brief or just to sound good, it is successful. The schema is a scaffold, not a strict rule.

TASK

Now that you have the tools to manipulate texture to create interest and variety, return to your score from **Part II**.

- Make a final decision on which instrument(s) you are writing for (piano, string quartet, piano plus one, or a different combination entirely).
- Using your schemata as guideposts, vary the texture only when a new schema is introduced and/or when a previous idea returns.

Do the musical ideas develop? ✓

Does the piece demonstrate good control of musical elements? ✓

RESPONDING TO A COMPOSITION BRIEF

In the previous chapters we have explored how to shape musical phrases, how those phrases combine into larger forms, and how texture and embellishment bring them to life. This chapter brings those strands together by showing how a composition brief can be used as a practical starting point – guiding musical choices from the first sketch through to a coherent, finished piece.

To achieve this, we will work through a three-step process:

1. Identify the key features of the brief
2. Use these features to define the musical character
3. Build a schematic pathway

Each step focuses on a distinct aspect of moving from brief to composition, and together they provide a flexible framework that can be adapted to a wide range of contexts.

Step 1: Identify the key features of the brief

Take a look at your brief and consider any clues that might point towards genre, occasion, mood, and instrumentation.

Composition brief	Genre	Occasion	Mood	Instrumentation
Compose a piece in rondo form for a classical music festival	Classical – rondo form	Classical music festival	Rondo movements are often lively and upbeat	Piano / solo instrument with piano accompaniment
Write an instrumental solo with accompaniment to be performed at a school concert	Brief implies a classical style	School concert	Could be reflective, declamatory, upbeat or dramatic	Solo instrument with piano accompaniment
Compose a musical theatre solo for a character waiting for their loved one to return	Musical Theatre	Narrative context provided by the brief	Pensive, anticipatory, yearning, sad	Vocal solo with keyboard or small band accompaniment
Compose a jazz ballad for a mixed ensemble of 2–4 players to be performed at a jazz festival	Jazz ballad	Jazz festival	Could be expressive, melancholy, wistful etc.	At minimum, solo instrument plus accompaniment; often includes bass and/or drums (e.g. two melody instruments, piano, drums)

The following example shows how the three-step process might be used when considering the second brief:

Write an instrumental solo with accompaniment to be performed at a school concert.

Instrumentation: solo violin and piano

- While the brief allows freedom, a solo violin provides a lyrical voice that stands out clearly in a school concert setting.
- Piano is a practical choice for the accompanying instrument and balances well with a solo violin.
- A small-ensemble accompaniment could be used but piano keeps the texture simple and focused.

Genre: Classical style

- A solo instrument plus accompaniment lends itself to a Classical style.
- No text or external narrative is provided; this implies a clear, self-contained musical form.

Occasion: School concert

- The piece is intended for performance at a school concert.
- School concerts typically accommodate a wide range of styles, moods, and genres.

Mood: A reflective piece to suit the lyrical tone of the violin

- As no specific mood is given, this provides freedom to choose the character of the piece.
- The school concert setting makes a reflective piece ideal for the middle of the program.

Step 2: Use these features to define the musical character

The findings from Step 1 have helped to suggest some initial ideas, which you can now use to make choices around tempo, metre, key, texture, and form.

These musical parameters can combine into something that is called a **topic** – a clear musical character or style that helps shape your piece. Here are some established musical topics that help to provide a starting point for a composition in the Classical style:

Topic	Tempo	Metre	Rhythm	Tonality
March	Fast (Allegro) or moderately fast (Allegro moderato)	$\frac{2}{4}$	Regular and predictable with some dotted rhythms for interest	Can be major or minor
Minuet	Moderate (Andante) or moderately fast.	$\frac{3}{4}$	Beat 1 is strong, beats 2 and 3 are weaker	Can be major or minor
Saraband	Slow (Largo or Larghetto)	$\frac{3}{4}$	Emphasis on beat 2	Major or minor
Jig	Fast	$\frac{6}{8}$ or $\frac{12}{8}$	Lively quaver motion	Major or minor
Pastorella	Moderately slow	$\frac{6}{8}$ or $\frac{12}{8}$	Lilting quaver motion with some dotted rhythms	Usually major, especially F major or B flat major

We can use similar parameters to guide our initial choices for genres outside of the Classical tradition:

Topic	Tempo	Metre	Musical features
Pop ballad	Moderate or moderately slow	4/4 or compound metre e.g. 12/8; 3/4 sometimes appears	**Harmony:** Mostly diatonic, functional. **Melody:** Lyrical, singable, emotive, and mainly stepwise with a few leaps. **Texture:** Typically sparse accompaniment during verses, fuller in choruses; emphasis on vocals.
Pop/rock song	Moderate or moderately fast	4/4 or 12/8 (sometimes called a 'shuffle')	**Harmony:** Mostly diatonic using chords in root position. **Melody:** Catchy, memorable; chorus often higher energy than verses. **Texture:** Melody (vocals), harmony (guitar/keyboard), and bass (bass guitar).
Jazz standard	Any, but usually moderate	4/4, but irregular metres e.g. 5/4 also appear	**Harmony:** Rich, extended chords; functional, goal-directed bass motion or a walking bass. **Melody:** Stepwise with chromatic embellishments and some leaps; motifs often used flexibly or repetitively. **Texture:** Small combo or big band; interplay between rhythm section and melody/horns.
Film score – military/patriotic/heroic	Steady or moderately fast	4/4	**Harmony:** Major keys, diatonic, primarily root position. **Melody:** Bold, soaring, clear, aspirational, fanfares and ascending motifs. **Texture:** Full orchestral; prominent brass and percussion.
Film score – action	Fast	4/4 or compound metre e.g. 12/8. Sometimes irregular metres are used (e.g., 5/8 or 7/8) to produce a dynamic, unbalanced effect.	**Harmony:** Minor or modal; tension-building dissonances. **Melody:** Aggressive, short, repetitive motifs; ostinatos. **Texture:** Thick, layered orchestration; emphasis on percussion, brass, and low strings.
Film score – sadness/romance	Slow	4/4 or compound metre e.g. 12/8	**Harmony:** Minor or major with modal mixture; extended chords, suspensions for emotional depth. **Melody:** Long, lyrical lines; expressive leaps; emotive phrasing. **Texture:** Strings, piano, woodwinds; delicate orchestration.
Film score – horror	Any	4/4, but often without a regular beat. Could also explore less conventional metres e.g. 7/8	**Harmony:** Dissonant, chromatic, atonal clusters; minor keys; tritones and diminished sonorities. **Melody:** Disjunct, unpredictable, fragmented; short, unsettling motifs. **Texture:** Sparse or extreme orchestral colours; unconventional sounds; high-pitched strings, percussive effects, eerie electronics.

Let's consider how this might apply to our example composition brief:

Write an instrumental solo with accompaniment to be performed at a school concert

In Step 1, we decided on a reflective piece for solo violin and piano to be played during the middle of a school concert. Looking at the Classical topics, a **minuet** would be a good fit here. The **minuet** topic helps us to decide on **tempo** (moderate), **metre** $\frac{3}{4}$, **key** (we'll choose an open string major – D major), and **form** (minuet and trio).

Musical choices for the other composition briefs might look something like this:

Composition brief	Topic
Compose a piece in rondo form for a classical music festival	Using Mozart's *Rondo Alla Turca* for inspiration, we might use the **march** topic to inform our choices: • Allegro tempo • $\frac{2}{4}$ metre • Minor key • Use of regular and dotted rhythms
Compose a musical theatre solo for a character waiting for their loved one to return	The yearning, sad mood suggests the **pop ballad** topic would work well: • Moderate tempo • $\frac{4}{4}$ metre • B flat major key (works well for a mezzo soprano range) • 32-bar song form (a type of ternary form)
Compose a jazz ballad for a mixed ensemble of 2–4 players to be performed at a jazz festival	**Jazz standard** topic is the obvious choice: • We might choose trumpet, piano, bass, and a drum kit • Moderate tempo • $\frac{4}{4}$ metre • B flat major (flat keys help our transposing instruments) • Ternary form is a good fit

Step 3 Build a schematic pathway

Once you have decided on the type of piece you would like to compose you'll need a schematic plan, like a scaffold, that you can use as a starting point to build on. We have seen some of these during the course of the book, but there are plenty more possibilities that have been tried and tested.

You can find a catalogue of schemata we haven't yet covered in **Appendix 2**, and examples of schematic pathways to try in **Appendix 3**.

Schemata give you a clear starting point, turning the blank page into a space full of possibilities, whatever the genre or style. One reliable approach is to use the musical form you've chosen to structure your piece, then refer to the relevant part of the toolkit to suggest a schematic starting point:

Write an instrumental solo with accompaniment to be performed at a school concert

This brief allows us plenty of freedom with schematic pathways. As we've decided on a minuet, we'll refer back to Part II to build our composition using the following schematic plan for a **minuet and trio**.

Minuet

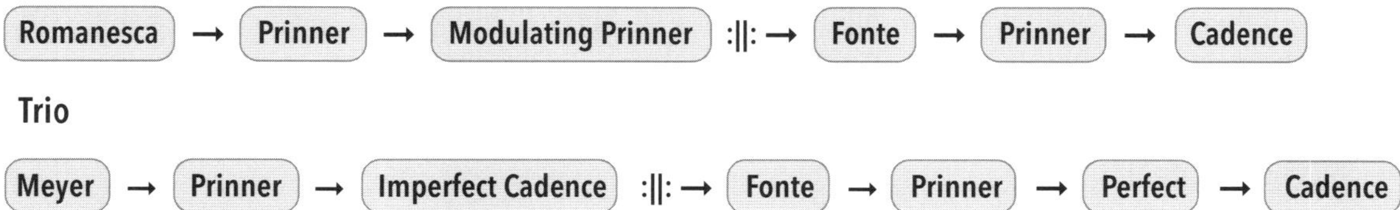

Trio

Meyer → Prinner → Imperfect Cadence :||: → Fonte → Prinner → Perfect → Cadence

This table shows which part of the toolkit to refer to when determining your schematic pathway for other example briefs:

Composition brief	Where to look
Compose a piece in rondo form for a classical music festival	Beginning of Part II: **Rondo form** **A:** Romanesca–Prinner **B** and **C:** Meyer, Do-Re-Mi, and/or Quiescenza in other keys (e.g. sub-dominant, dominant, or relative minor)
Compose a musical theatre solo for a character waiting for their loved one to return	Part I: **Romanesca**; **Prinner**; Part II: **Quiescenza** (with additional information taken from the table of **musical topics** earlier in this chapter) • Starting with a 'standing still' Quiescenza would help set the scene of waiting for someone • Descending shape of the Romanesca is also suitable as it suggests nostalgia • Prinner – Cadence progression shows resolution or renewed hope • Keep harmonic rhythm slower for lyrical delivery • Use an ascending Monte (see Appendix 2) to suggest hope, expectation, or anxiety
Compose a jazz ballad for a mixed ensemble of 2–4 players to be performed at a jazz festival	Beginning of Part II: **Ternary Form in Popular Music** **Head** (A): Adapt the Romanesca–Prinner pattern with jazz harmonies (added 7ths, 9ths etc.) **Bridge** (B): Use the Fonte or extended Prinner with flexible rhythm and enriched harmony

With musical choices decided and explored, you should now be able to draw on the toolkit we've added to throughout the book to support these choices with elaboration of melody, rhythm, and texture to develop your composition while maintaining interest and contrast.

And finally…

Over the course of this book, we have explored the building blocks of composition considering schemata, form, texture, and elaboration. Composing is both a structural and creative process – while the schemata provide guidance, the composer's choices ultimately shape the character and style of the music. Schemata provide building blocks for a composer to create interesting melodies, strong and supportive bass lines, and passages that move logically from one section to the next, allowing ideas to grow and unfold in a way that makes musical sense.

Let's take a final look at the criteria for what makes a good composition, and consider how the ideas in this book support them:

- Does the melody have a clear, recognisable line? ✓

- Does the melody move in steps with occasional leaps? ✓

- Does the melody have some rhythmic variety to keep it interesting? ✓

- Is there a clear bass line that underpins the melody? ✓

- Is there a combination of similar and contrary motion between the melody and bass lines? ✓

- Is there a clear sense of harmony? ✓

- Does the piece have some contrasting material? ✓

- Is the structure clear and coherent, with convincing musical progression? ✓

- Do the musical ideas develop? ✓

- Does the piece demonstrate good control of musical elements? ✓

Step by step, from sketch to finished score, a toolkit of compositional techniques combined with thoughtful choices at every stage can produce music that is well-crafted and compelling.

APPENDIX 1

Working examples

PART I: Complete rounded binary form using Romanesca, Prinner, and Fonte

PART II: Complete ternary form

Complete minuet and trio form

Rondo form

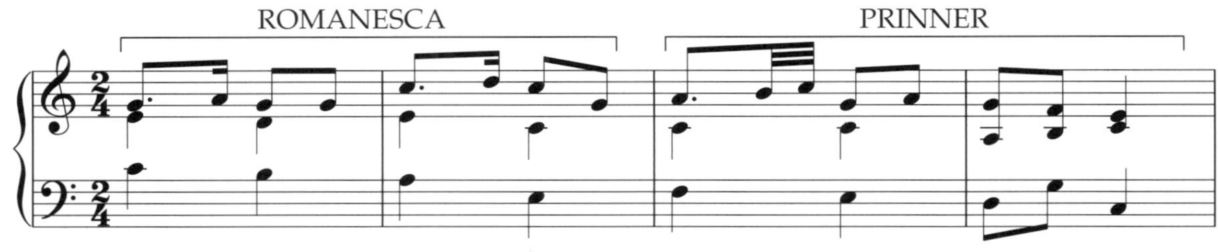

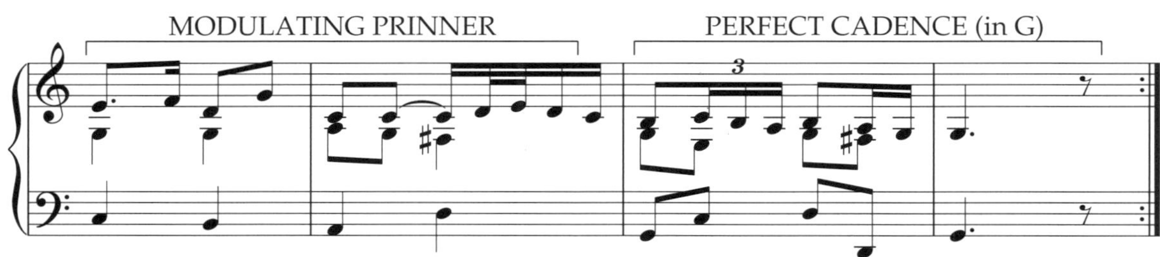

PRINNER
PERFECT CADENCE
ROMANESCA
PRINNER
MODULATING PRINNER
PERFECT CADENCE (in G)
3
FONTE
PRINNER
PERFECT CADENCE (in C)
DO-RE-MI

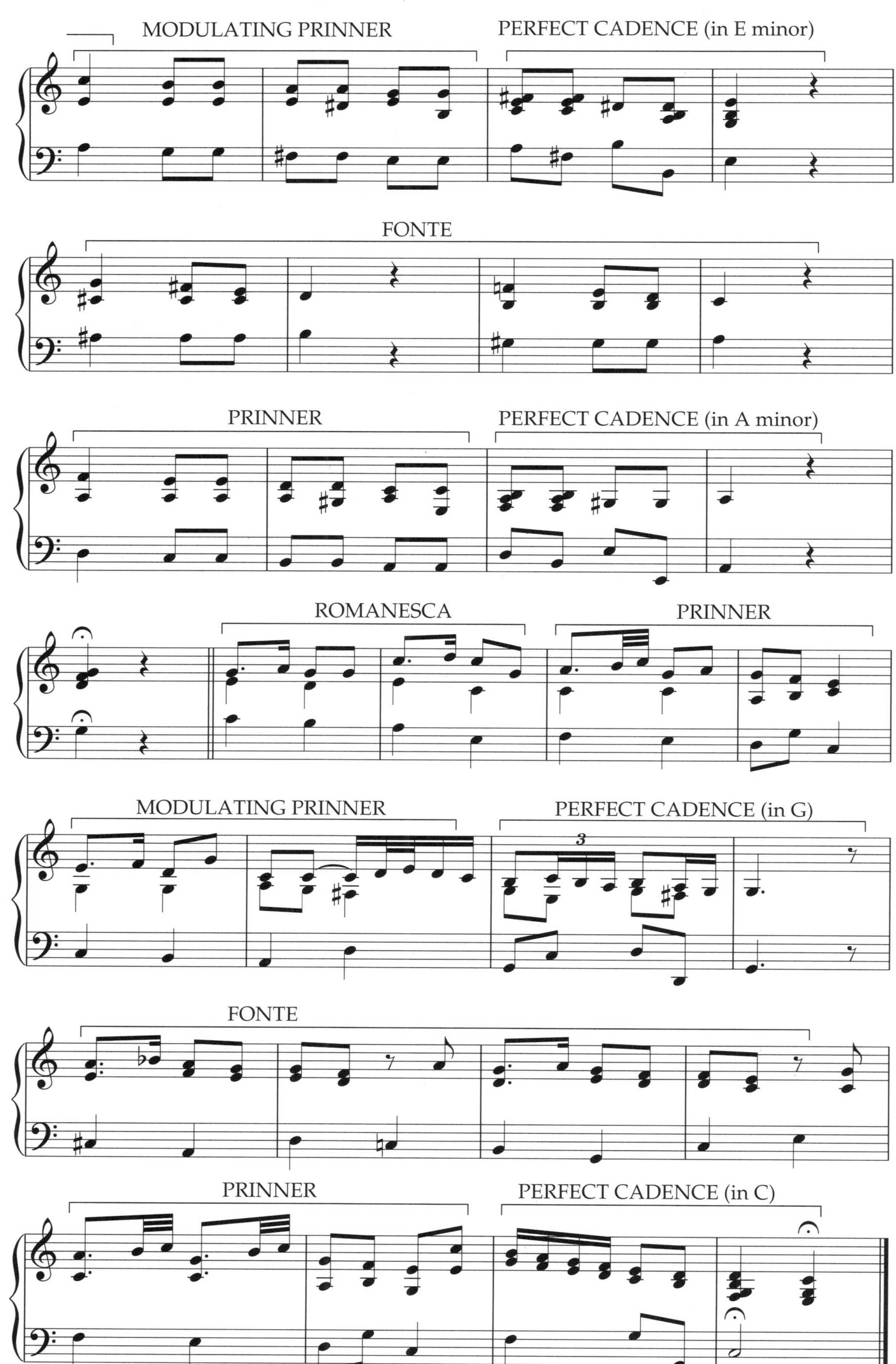

MODULATING PRINNER
PERFECT CADENCE (in E minor)
FONTE
PRINNER
PERFECT CADENCE (in A minor)
ROMANESCA
PRINNER
MODULATING PRINNER
PERFECT CADENCE (in G)
FONTE
PRINNER
PERFECT CADENCE (in C)

APPENDIX 2: CATALOGUE OF ADDITIONAL SCHEMATA

This appendix covers the remaining schemata that have not been discussed in detail during the course of the book but may be useful for elaborating your compositions. The ideas presented here are somewhat more advanced than those presented in earlier chapters and are intended as an invitation for you to experiment and improvise with. For a comprehensive index of all the galant schemata, please see Robert O. Gjerdingen's online resource at *https://partimenti.org/schemas/collections/galant/schema_prototypes.pdf.*

SOL-FA-MI

Melody: ❺-❹|❹-❸

Bass: ①-②|⑦-①

This is similar to the Do-Re-Mi schema. It is another common opening gesture, but the main difference is that the melody approaches ❸ from above rather than from below. Like the Do-Re-Mi, it is usually divided into four events rather than three. See the Haydn *Minuet* example, bars 1–4. on page 76.

Mozart – "Non più andrai" from *Figaro* [Anna Netrebko / Ildebrando D'arcangelo: [0:00–0:10]

Abba – *I Have a Dream* [0:31–0:49]

What I Did for Love from *A Chorus Line* (Marvin Hamlisch) [0:13–0:25]

PONTE

The word 'Ponte' means 'bridge' in Italian, and that's a great way to think about this schema: a musical bridge that extends the phrase and builds anticipation for what comes next. The Ponte is most commonly found after a structural arrival on ⑤: an imperfect cadence. The bass line sits on ⑤ while the upper voices remain active, decorating the dominant harmony. This creates a specific musical effect. Even though the music is still moving on the surface, nothing is really advancing in terms of harmony. In other words, it feels as though the music is treading water.

Unlike most other schemata, the Ponte isn't based on a fixed melodic shape. Its purpose is to prolong the dominant: think of it as a passage of dominant harmony, where the dominant chord is held and explored in different ways. Despite this flexibility, there are two common strategies composers use to write a Ponte.

1. Using notes from the dominant (or dominant 7th) chord

The first strategy is to use the notes of the dominant chord (or dominant 7th) over a **pedal** (repeated or sustained notes) on ⑤. This is very straightforward to do, and it can instantly create a sense of tension and buildup to the beginning of a new passage of music. The Classical approach is to ascend through the notes of the dominant 7th in the melody. Composers therefore tend to emphasise the 'Ponte tones' in the melody (i.e., the notes of the scale belonging to the dominant 7th): ❷, ❹, ❺, and ❼.

2. Alternating between root-position and second-inversion chords

The second strategy still uses a static pedal on ⑤, but instead of only using the notes of the dominant 7th (❷,❹,❺, and ❼) it alternates between root-position (5/3) and second inversion (6/4). This type of Ponte can stretch out the dominant harmony over several bars, making it especially effective after an imperfect cadence as a way of prolonging the suspense (see Mozart *Sonata in C* bars 11–12 on page 75.

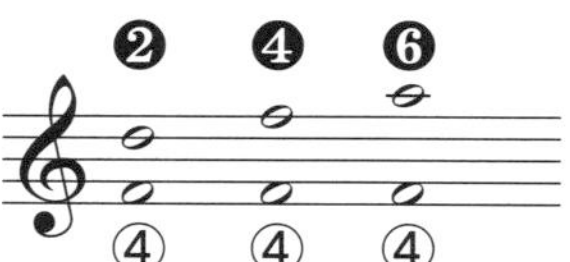

INDUGIO

Melody: ❷-❹-❻…etc.

Bass: ④-④-④…etc.

While the Ponte prolongs an imperfect cadence after it occurs, the Indugio delays a cadence before it arrives. The Italian word 'indugio' translates as 'delay', 'lateness', or even 'procrastination', and that is exactly the effect it creates in music.

In a typical galant phrase, the music often moves deliberately towards ⑤, either half-closing there with an imperfect cadence or continuing to ① to produce a perfect cadence. The Indugio blocks that motion by lingering on ④, delaying the arrival (Mozart *Sonata in C*, bars 9–10 on p.75; see also Haydn *Minuet* No.11, bars 5–6 on p.76). ④ in the bass usually supports a root-position harmony, though it can be enriched with a dissonant chord in 6/5/3 position.

At its core, the Indugio creates a kind of musical hesitation or suspense, but not in a way that feels passive. Instead, it usually builds up energy, like static electricity waiting to discharge. While the basic job of an Indugio is to remain on ④, there are two main ways to exit from the schema. One is just to move straight to ⑤ (see the Haydn), but the more stylish way would be to move to ⑤ chromatically through #④ (see Mozart).

- Mozart – *Piano Sonata No. 1 in C Major*, K. 279: I. Allegro [Maria João Pires 0:52–1:02]

- Haydn – *Symphony No. 60 in C Major*, Hob. I:60 "Il distratto": I. Adagio – Allegro di molto [Seiji Ozawa 2:01–2:14]

- Beyoncé – *Halo* [3:22–3:28]

FENAROLI

Melody: ❹-❸-❼-❶

Bass: ⑦-①-②-③

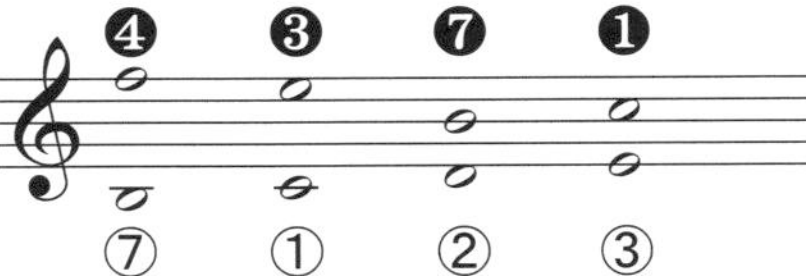

Like the Ponte and Indugio, the **Fenaroli** schema is used to delay the progress of a piece of music to make it last longer. Of any schema, the Fenaroli gives the strongest impression of the music treading water. It can be used to expand the tonic in any given passage, just like the Ponte prolongs ⑤ and the Indugio prolongs ④. The main difference, however, is that the Fenaroli is made from a fixed bass line over which a small group of melodic choices can be selected. The bass nearly always uses the notes ⑦-①-②-③ while the most common melodic pattern is ❹-❸-❼-❶.

While the Fenaroli works perfectly well in this format, variations are available. It is possible for both the bass line and the melodic line to use the same degrees of the scale but starting at a different point, creating a **canon**: ❷-❸-❼-❶ in the melody against ⑦-①-②-③ in the bass line. The continuous nature of this helps to give the Fenaroli its characteristic cyclic motion which is especially effective when played twice in a row. In any of these examples, the addition of an inner voice repeating ❺ is characteristic.

- Schubert – *String Quintet No. 6 in G Major*: I. Allegro [Karl Ditters von Ditterdorf (Julius Berger, cello) 0:43–0:51]

- Queen – *Love of My Life* [0:00–0:08]

THE MONTE

Melody: ❺-❹-❸ up a step → ❺-❹-❸

Bass: ⑦ - ①   ⑦ - ①

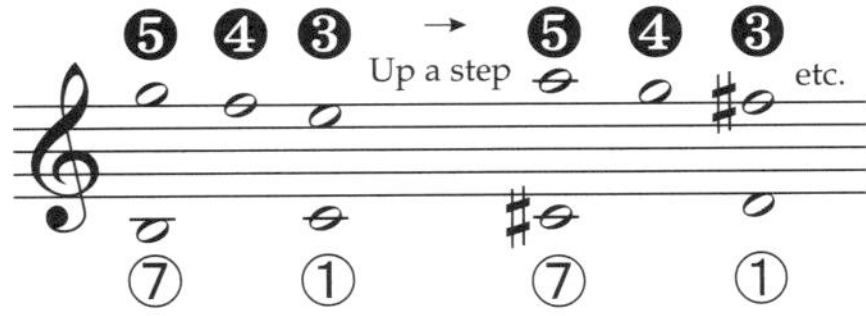

Sometimes you might not want your music to stand still. Many of the schemata that we have considered have featured descending patterns (Romanesca, Prinner, Fonte), which are useful for resolving tension with their reassuring descents towards tonic harmony. Sometimes, though, composers working in the galant style wanted to produce the opposite effect: an increase in tension and drama. The corresponding ascending motion of the Monte schema was popular with galant composers for this reason, and this is where it gets its name from ('monte' is Italian for 'mountain', so this schema is like a mountain to climb).

Like the Fonte, it relies on a sequence, however, there are some important differences between the Fonte and the Monte.

1. Where the Fonte relies on a *descending* sequence (usually from ii to I), the Monte is based on an *ascending* sequence

2. Where the Fonte usually happens in only two stages, the Monte has no specific limit to the number of times composers would repeat the upward sequential motion. A simple Monte might, for example, move from IV to V before the composer introduces a new schema. There are longer examples, though, in which the Monte goes through 3, 4, 5 or even more stages.

Vivaldi – *L'estro armonico*, Violin Concerto in G Major, RV 310, Op. 3 No. 3: I. Allegro [Simon Standage / The English Concert / Trevor Pinnock 0:14–0:23]

Vivaldi – *The Four Seasons*, Autumn, Violin Concerto in F Major, RV 293, Op. 8 No. 3: III. La caccia. Allegro [Janine Jansen 0:57–1:08]

Queen – *Flash*: [1:00–1:09]

OTHER TYPES OF CADENCE

The Passo Indietro

Melody: ❼-❶

Bass: ④-③

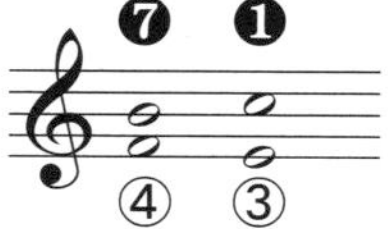

This is Italian for a 'step back', and it does exactly what its name suggests – the music appears to retreat just before reaching a cadence. Specifically, the bass moves in the wrong direction – from ④ to ③. In this scenario, ④ supports a dominant 7th in 6/4/2 position (a third inversion), which then resolves to a tonic chord in 6/3 position (first inversion) over ③. The result is a cadence that *sounds* as though it's heading for closure but instead sidesteps it, pressing pause just before the music can land properly.

The sense of the music 'going backwards' can be a very effective tool for extending a phrase. Because the cadence sounds correct yet incomplete, the music can then 'try again' a few bars later, perhaps using the Passo Indietro once more or following it with an interrupted cadence, while deciding the right time to progress towards a perfect cadence.

Nielsen – *Symphony No. 1 in G Minor*, Op. 7: II. Andante [John Storgårds / BBC Philharmonic 5:12–5:24]

The Comma

Melody: **④**-**❸**

Bass: ⑦-①

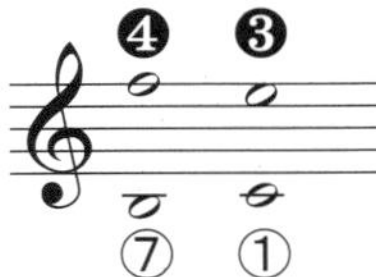

Another example of a weaker cadence is the **Comma**. Like the Passo Indietro, it involves a motion from V-I, but again the chords are inverted which makes it feel less final. In this case the bass voice moves from ⑦ to ① while the melody moves from ❹ to ❸. By avoiding landing on ❶ in the melody, the impact is softened. The Comma cadence is therefore useful in the middle of a phrase to weakly round off part of an idea before continuing to develop it, or it can be used to suggest a key before fully confirming it with a perfect cadence using root-position chords.

 Mozart – *Piano Sonata No. 16 in C Major*, K545: I. Allegro [Christian Blackshaw 0:07–0:09]

The Clausula Vera

Melody: **❼**-**❶**

Bass: ②-①

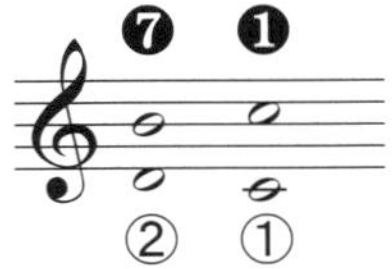

The last example of a cadence that weakly articulates a key is the **Clausula Vera** (meaning a 'true close'). In this cadence the bass moves from ② to ① while the melody usually moves either from ❼ to ❶ or from ❹ to ❸. Although it was used commonly in early music, it is quite rare to find this cadence at the end of a piece of classical music (the beautiful Adagietto from Mahler's Fifth Symphony uses a tonic-key *Clausula Vera* right at the end, but this is a notable exception). However, it is extremely common to find a Clausula Vera onto the key of the dominant, and this is nearly always followed by a Ponte.

Haydn – Symphony No. 78 in C Minor, Hob.I:78–1. Vivace [Accademia Bizantina / Ottavio Dantone 0:42–0:44]

Mahler – Symphony No. 5 in C-Sharp Minor: IV. Adagietto. Sehr langsam [Simon Rattle / Berlin Philharmoniker 9:00–end]

APPENDIX 3: SCHEMATIC PATHWAYS

This appendix outlines various different pathways you could follow when bringing together schemata into a musical structure. This is by no means an exhaustive list. As with everything else in the book, treat them as a starting point to help you overcome the hurdle of the blank page. If your improvisations lead you somewhere else, go with it!

Here's a quick reminder of the different schemata – your building blocks – and where you might use them.

Schema	Function	Where to put it structurally
Romanesca	Explores tonic key	Opening / main theme
Do-Re-Mi	Stepwise melodic ascent	Opening / main theme
Sol-Fa-Mi	Stepwise melodic descent	Opening / main theme
Quiescenza	Standing still	Opening / main theme, after structural cadence or in a codetta
Prinner (on I)	Response, moves towards tonic	Response or middle B section in 32-bar song form
Prinner (on V)	Response, modulates to dominant	Transition
Fonte	Sequential descent	Middle
Monte	Ascending sequence	Middle / development
Fenaroli	Decorative fill; contrasting theme (in new key)	Middle / elaboration
Indugio	Delays cadence	Before cadence
Ponte	Builds anticipation	Preparation for return to tonic

Here are some examples of pathways you can construct with them:

1. Basic binary form with modulation to V and return to I

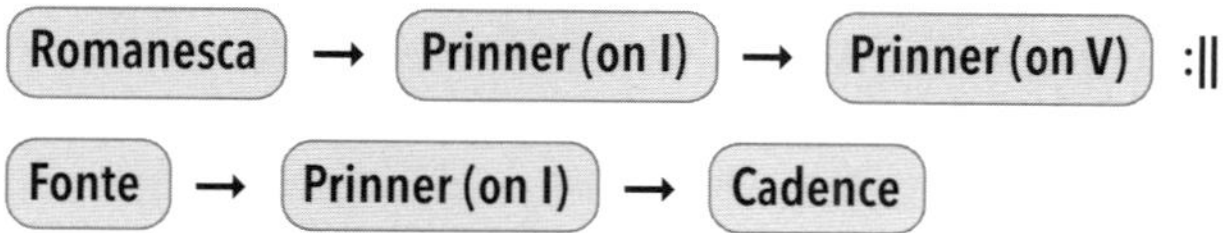

You could use this scaffold to create something completely new by varying the tempo, metre, key, and instrumentation. Try to make your piece sound as different as possible from our example while still using the same schemata.

2. More complex binary using Indugio and Ponte

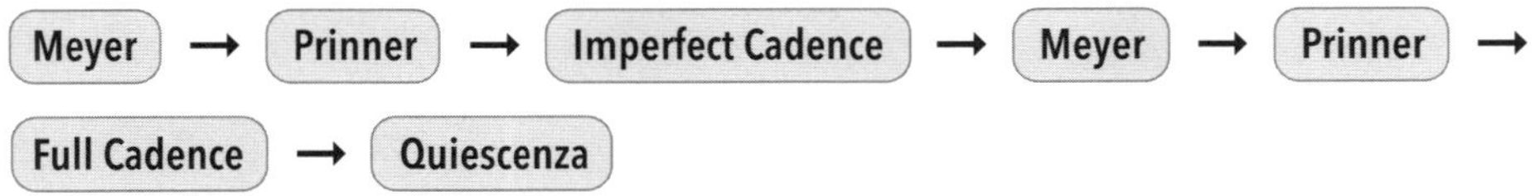

This pathway is a little more extensive than the first. See how long you can make your Indugio last without it losing momentum. See **Appendix 2** for the Indugio and Ponte schemas.

3. A balanced statement with structural cadences and codetta

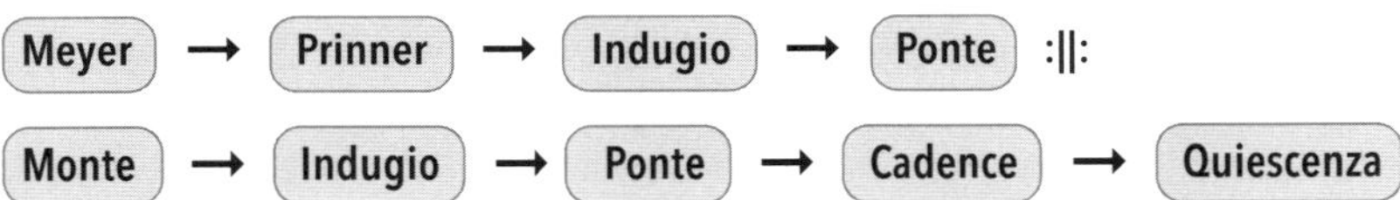

This pathway creates a sort of symmetrical structure – a musical **period** – with an imperfect cadence in the middle and a perfect cadence at the end. Notice that the Quiescenza only comes after the cadence. Since this makes for quite a short piece, you could try turning it into a relatively straightforward theme and then compose a series of variations with ever more ornate decorations.

4. Binary form with dramatic Monte in the middle

In this schematic plan the space after the double bar, which is usually occupied by the Fonte schema, is replaced with the Monte. This could be quite exciting, especially at a faster tempo. This also invites a more energetic texture to go with the musical energy that the Monte brings.

5. A straightforward sonata exposition

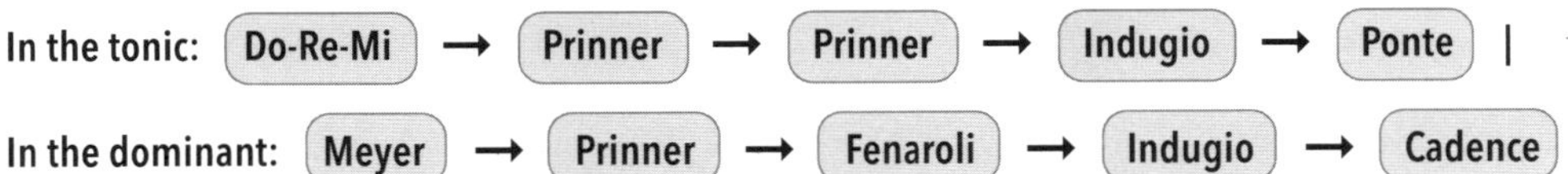

This schematic pathway is in two parts. The first is in the tonic key and it arrives on dominant harmony with a Ponte at the end. The second part is in the dominant key, and it closes in that key. This pathway begins in one key and ends in another, and it therefore begins to take on the characteristics of a **sonata exposition**. If you were also to repeat the process with both parts in the tonic key then you would have composed a **recapitulation**, and therefore an entire sonata form. For more information on **sonata form**, please see *The Symphony: From Mannheim to Mahler* (Tarrant and Wild, 2022).

GLOSSARY

Term	Definition
Alberti bass	A broken-chord accompaniment pattern (typically low-high-middle-high) commonly used in eighteenth-century keyboard music as part of a melody and accompaniment texture.
Appoggiatura	A dissonant melodic note occurring on the beat that resolves by step, usually downwards, to the next consonant note.
Arpeggiation	Leaping motion using only the notes of the chord.
Augmented 6th	A predominant chord: the bass moves down from the flattened submediant to the dominant (♭6 → 5); the upper voice moves up from the sharpened subdominant to the dominant (♯4 → 5).
Bass line	The lowest voice in the texture.
Binary form	A piece in two sections, usually separated by a double barline. The first section moves away from the tonic to establish a new key and the second returns to and confirms the initial tonic. Both sections are usually repeated.
Cadence	A form of musical punctuation. Cadences articulate the end point of sections of music and whole musical forms.
Cadential deferral	The process by which tonal closure is postponed to a later stage in a piece of music.
Chromatic	A way of describing music that uses notes outside of its key.
Coda	A passage of music that occurs after the end of a musical form (such as a rondo or ternary form). Its function is to frame or to round off an already completed musical form.
Codetta	A short passage of music that comes immediately after a structural cadence, typically making use of the Quiescenza schema.
Comma cadence	A relatively weak cadence where the bass moves from ⑦ to ① and the melody moves from ❹ to ❸.
Conjunct	A way of describing music that moves primarily by steps as opposed to leaps.
Conservatory	A school dedicated to teaching music (French, *conservatoire*; Italian, *conservatorio*).
Consonance	A harmonic interval of a unison, 3rd, perfect 5th, 6th, octave, or their compounds (intervals larger than an octave built from these). A perfect 4th is consonant only between two upper voices; it is dissonant when it is between any voice and the bass.
Contrary motion	When two or more musical voices move in the opposite direction from one another.
Counterpoint	A texture in which two or more melodies move independently of each other.

Cudworth cadence	A typical galant cadence in which the melody descends through a whole octave over ④-⑤-① in the bass.
Da Capo al Fine	An instruction asking the player(s) to go back to the beginning and play through to where '*fine*' is marked.
Diatonic	A way of describing music that uses notes belonging to a given key or mode.
Diminished 7th	A stack of four notes, each separated by a minor 3rd.
Disjunct	A way of describing music that moves primarily by leaps as opposed to steps.
Dissonance	A harmonic interval of a 2nd, tritone, or 7th, or any of their compounds (intervals larger than an octave built from these). A perfect 4th is dissonant only when it is between the bass and another voice.
Do-Re-Mi	A schema featuring the rising melody ❶-❷-❸
Dominant	The fifth degree of the key (or the triad built on that note).
Double appoggiatura	Two appoggiaturas that resolve together, typically a 6/4 dissonance resolving to a 5/3 chord.
Evaded cadence	A cadence where the melody suggests resolution to ❶, but then moves evasively, usually to ❸ or ❺.
Fanfare	A musical topic, thematic idea, or whole piece that relies heavily on arpeggiated motion, commonly for brass instruments.
First inversion	A chord position in which the third note of the scale is at the bass of the triad, producing a 6/3 chord.
Fonte	A schema comprising a descending sequence in two stages, first in the supertonic minor then a step lower in the tonic major. The Fonte is often found immediately after the central double bar in galant binary forms.
Galant style	An elegant, urbane, courtly musical style in the mid-eighteenth century that relied on a collection of recognised patterns known as 'schemata'.
Harmony	The combination of notes played together as chords, and how those chords are used to support the melody and shape the music.
Homophony	A musical texture in which all voices move together to make a series of chords.
Idiomatic	Writing that suits a particular style or is well-established for a particular instrument or group of instruments.
Improvisation	The act of creating music without preparation. In the galant style, this process usually starts with a basic shape to improvise on: a schema.
Imperfect cadence	An arrival at the end of a musical statement on a root-position V chord that feels unfinished, making the music want to continue.

Indugio	A musical schema that lingers on the subdominant chord.
Interrupted cadence	Also sometimes called a 'deceptive cadence', the music appears to be moving towards a perfect cadence, but instead of resolving to the tonic, it moves to the submediant (usually chord vi), creating a sense of derailment.
Jazz standard	A popular song form that is a core part of the jazz repertoire. The ternary (aaba) 'head' of the song becomes the object of improvisation by the instrumentalists.
Jig	A fast dance form in compound metre (usually 6/8) found in the Baroque and folk repertoires.
Key	The system of notes and chords a piece of music is based on, with one note as the main "home" (the tonic).
Leading note	The seventh degree of the diatonic scale.
Mannheim Roller	A musical effect used by the Mannheim school in the eighteenth century and later assimilated into orchestral works across Europe: a rising melody heard over a tonic pedal combined with a crescendo to build tension.
March	A moderate or fast piece of music in duple metre.
Melody	The main, upper voice in a musical texture.
Melody and accompaniment	A musical texture that foregrounds a single melodic voice, supported by chordal accompaniment.
Melisma	The setting of several notes per single syllable of text in vocal music, often for expression, ornamentation, or word painting.
Metre	The temporal structure of music. In the tonal repertoire this is usually expressed through a time signature.
Meyer	A schema used as an opening idea. It is expressed in two stages, the first creating tension and the second releasing it.
Minuet	A moderate, stately dance form that was common in the Baroque suite and the Classical symphony. Minuets are in triple metre (usually 3/4).
Minuet and Trio form	An eighteenth-century dance form in triple metre. It comprises contrasting sections arranged in ternary form (ABA).
Modulation	Motion from one key to another.
Monophony	A musical texture consisting of a single melodic line.
Mordent	A type of ornamentation in which the player briefly alternates the main note with the note above or below.
Motif	A short, memorable idea that returns throughout a piece of music.

Neapolitan 6th	A chord built on the flattened supertonic (2nd degree of the scale). This is always a major triad and is typically presented in first inversion.
Neighbouring note	A note either one tone or one semitone above or below the main note.
Ostinato	A repeated pattern.
Pastorella	A moderately slow dance form in compound metre (usually 6/8) evoking the peacefulness of nature.
Perfect cadence	A closing gesture where a V chord in root position moves to I, giving a strong sense of finality.
Polyphony	A musical texture in which two or more melodies move interdependently. The word 'polyphony' is commonly associated with early music; in the eighteenth century and later this kind of texture was referred to as 'counterpoint'.
Ponte	A galant schema that emphasises the fifth degree of the scale and dominant harmony. It is usually found immediately after an imperfect cadence.
Pop ballad	A slow, sentimental, or romantic song.
Prinner	A galant schema that is used as a riposte or a responding gesture.
Quiescenza	A galant schema that is commonly used either as an opening gesture or as a codetta.
Rhythmic elaboration	The use of rhythm to prolong a more basic musical shape.
Romanesca	A galant schema that is commonly used as an opening gesture in classical and popular genres.
Rondo form	A musical form usually used for a finale of a multi-movement work, characterised by frequent repetition of a main theme separated by episodes in contrasting keys.
Root position	A chord in which the lowest voice plays the tonic, or 'root'.
Rounded binary form	A two-part form in which the second section brings back the opening material before the end. It combines the tonal plan of binary form with a partial return of the opening, making it a common building block in larger structures such as minuets and rondos.
Saraband	A slow Baroque dance form in triple metre (usually 3/4, sometimes 3/2), with an emphasis on the second beat.
Scalic elaboration	The use of stepwise motion to add layers of decoration to a more basic musical shape.
Schema	A basic musical pattern that composers use as a foundation for elaboration and improvisation.
Second inversion	A chord position in which the fifth note of the scale is played by the lowest voice.
Secondary 7th	A dominant seventh chord that relates to a key other than the current tonic. Common examples are the dominant of the dominant (V/V) and the dominant of the relative minor (V/vi).

Similar motion	Two or more voices moving in the same direction (either ascending or descending).
Sol-Fa-Mi	A galant schema commonly found as an opening gesture.
Sonata	A multi-movement instrumental work, often for a solo instrument (frequently keyboard) or solo instrument with accompaniment, typically following Classical-era formal principles.
Subdominant	The fourth degree of the scale, or the chord that is built on the fourth scale degree.
Suspension	A dissonance that is created when a note is held over from a previous chord to the new chord before resolving.
Syncopation	A rhythmic effect created when notes are accented off the beat or held across strong beats, disrupting the expected pattern of accents.
Ternary form	A musical form in three sections: A–B–A. The first section (A) usually ends in the tonic key. The middle section (B) contrasts in key, mood, or material, before a return to the opening section, sometimes with slight changes or embellishments.
Tonic	The first degree of a key (or the chord built on it), serving as the main point of rest and reference in tonal music.
Topic	A combination of musical parameters such as key, tempo, and metre that create a recognisable character or style.
Triad	The first, third, and fifth degrees of the scale combined to make a chord.
Trill	A type of ornamentation in which the performer alternates repeatedly between the main note and the note above.
Variation form	A musical form in which an initial theme is repeated with gradual changes in melody, harmony, rhythm, or texture
Word painting	A technique in which the meaning of the words is reflected in the music.

Acknowledgements

As with composition, no one ever writes a book all on their own; there are always ideas and influences that are actively sought by the authors, or that arise through conversations with friends, colleagues, and students by the sheerest of accidents. In the first of these categories, we would like to thank the teachers and students from several schools in the North East of England and elsewhere in the UK who, whether they knew it or not, were acting as guinea pigs for the schematic approach to composition, which is now well established in universities but was until recently untested at school level. In the North East region the schools that participated in the formation of this book were: King's Priory (Tynemouth), Cardinal Hume (Gateshead), St Wilfred's (South Shields), Sacred Heart (Newcastle), and Royal Grammar School (Newcastle). Further afield, we worked with Stowe School (Buckinghamshire) and Waldegrave School (Twickenham). The many, and often repeated workshops were crucial to the development of the idea for this book. Workshops hosted at Newcastle University would not have been possible without the guiding influence of Jenny Williams from the North East Music Education Hub. Jenny is a force of nature with a flair for bringing the right people together.

We would like to thank the many teachers from across England who have generously given their time and feedback on this project. In particular we would like to thank all the music teachers working in Music in Secondary Schools Trust partner schools, as well as colleagues within the organisation, for their enthusiasm and trust. Particular thanks go to Stephanie Bissell, Emma Cunliffe, and David Rich.

Students at Newcastle University have become acquainted with schemata over several years now, and this area of theory has been part of the furniture in musical analysis classes. Their questions, responses, and insights have directly fed into the content of this book, and we thank them for their enthusiasm and curiosity. We also thank colleagues at Newcastle University, especially David Clarke, Julia Partington, Kirsten Gibson, Larry Zazzo, Bennett Hogg, and Eric Doughney for being a sounding board and providing some critical advice as the book was coming together.

Finally, we must thank several individuals for their specific input into this project. As primarily classical musicians, Gregory Felton's advice on where to find non-classical examples of schemata has been extremely valuable for us and has led to some fun realisations. Jonathan Gibson's assistance with the setting of musical examples, his technical knowledge of engraving software, and the generosity he has shown with his time, have been essential to ensuring the progress of the project when time was tight. We would like to thank Imogen Hall at Faber Music for her expertise and experience in producing the volume and making it as accessible and user-friendly as it is. Finally, we would like to thank Craig Lawton for the many lively conversations we have had on the contextualising philosophy behind schema theory, what it means to be a composer, and the nature of genius.